LIVERPOOL

LIVERPOOL

Mary Cathcart Borer

Illustrated by Paul Shardlow

Longman

LONGMAN GROUP LIMITED

LONDON

Associated companies, branches and
representatives throughout the world

First published 1971

ISBN 0 582 15047 7

14179

J942·72

Printed in Great Britain by
The Camelot Press Ltd
London and Southampton

CONTENTS

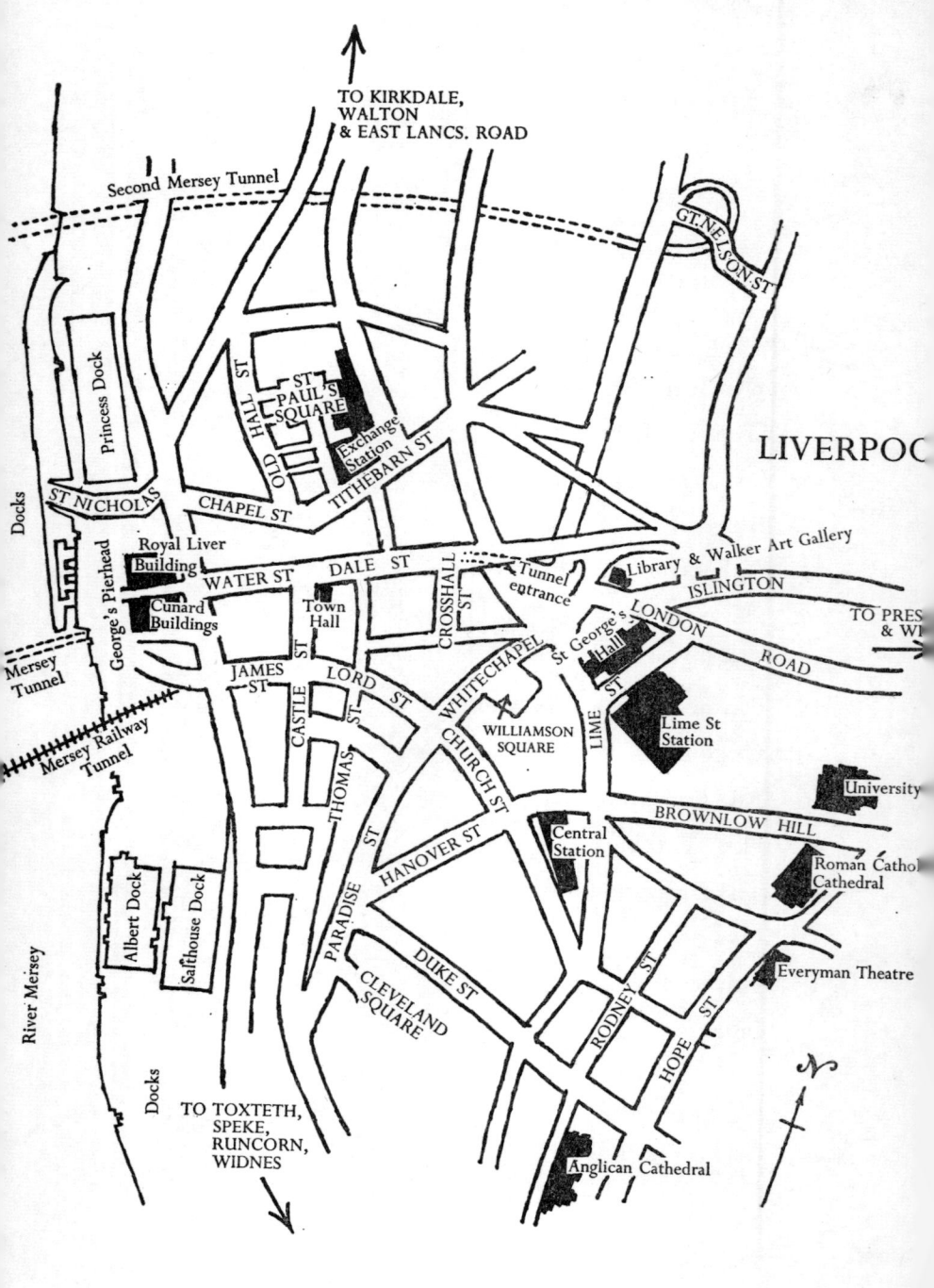

1. THE BEGINNINGS

When William of Normandy landed in England in 1066 he came to a lonely, remote country which was on the north-western fringe of the known world. It was a land of less than a million and a half people, most of whom were living in the south-eastern part of the country, where the climate was softer and the land rich and fertile.

The midlands of England were covered with dense oak and ash forests, haunted by wolves and wild boar, deer and wild oxen. On the uplands were great beechwoods and in the stretches of lowland in between were thick woods of elder, maple and lime. The weald of Kent was a dense forest, except for a few clearings made by the iron workers. The Essex marshes were a dreary, undrained malarial waste, almost entirely under water during the spring tides, and the fens of East Anglia and the marshes of Pevensey and Romney were little better, for nothing had been done about draining them since the last Romans had left the country, six hundred years earlier.

North-west of the midland forests, in what is now the county of Lancashire, there stretched, behind the wide expanse of sandy shores, mile after mile of bleak and desolate moorland, swamps and forests, the home of eagles and ravens, wolves, wild oxen, stags and roebuck. During the eighth century a few Norse fishermen had settled here, but they left few traces and vast tracts of land were still uninhabited.

England in 1066 was a primitive, pioneer country, her people still clearing the forest and scrub in order to create farmland. Each year a little more of the countryside came under cultivation, but the eleventh century was a slow-moving, hand-made world and by the time William I's Domesday Book was compiled, in 1086, there were still only 500,000 acres of cultivated land in England, compared with 19,000,000 acres in 1939.

In this quiet, solitary land, Lancashire was one of its most isolated regions, for it was cut off from the rest of the country by marshes to the north-east, the great bog of Chat Moss to the south-east and the Pennines to the east. Even the river Mersey and its short tributaries did not reach into the heart of the country, to provide a useful inland waterway, like the rivers of the south-east. The Mersey from its sources to the estuary at Runcorn is only forty miles long, while its main tributary, the Irwell, is even shorter. The network of Roman roads from London to the north-west ended at Chester, fifteen miles away, south of the Wirral peninsula, and the extension from Chester to Lancaster crossed the Mersey seventeen miles inland, at Warrington.

Lancashire had once been part of the old English kingdom of Strathclyde. Then it had passed to the Danish kingdom of Northumbria. It had been included in the kingdom of Mercia and then returned to Northumbria, before the English kingdoms had become united.

With the advent of the Normans and their feudal system, the old English earldoms were abolished and most of the nobility dispossessed. The country was divided into counties, each of which was governed by a sheriff. The counties were divided into areas called "hundreds" and the hundreds sub-divided into regions or "manors".

King William kept about a quarter of England's land for himself and the remainder he divided between some hundred and fifty of his "Companions", most of whom had accompanied him on the 1066 campaign. Some became lords of seven or eight hundred manors. Less important men may have had twenty manors or even less. In return, these Norman barons promised to raise an army for the King when it was needed, and in order to do this they parcelled out their land to subtenants and the sub-tenants to smallholders and peasants or "villeins", who were legally bound to join the barons' armies when the demand came.

The King defended his new kingdom with great stone castles. He ordered them to be built at every county town throughout the country and at the important ports, and he allowed his barons to build private castles to defend the estates he had bestowed on them.

There is no mention of a settlement at Liverpool in the Domesday Book. In fact the county of Lancashire is not represented at all. The flat, marshy country between the Ribble and the Mersey was surveyed with Cheshire, and the country to the north of the Ribble was included with Yorkshire.

Among the new earldoms created by William I, the earldom of Chester was given to Hugh of Avranches and the earldom of Shrewsbury to Roger of Montgomery. Roger of Poictou, another member of the Montgomery family, was allotted land to the north of the Mersey estuary and before long became lord of the county of Lancaster.

One of the hundreds of Roger of Poictou's land was West Derby, this area stretching from about where Southport now stands down to the Mersey and inland as far as the site of Wigan. The Domesday commissioners reported that there were more clearings and settlements in this part of the county than elsewhere. They recorded sixty-six, but this represented only three thousand people, and nine tenths of West Derby was still waste land. Each settlement can have been little more than eight or ten cottages—single-roomed, roughly-made shelters of clay or stone—dark, dismal, unhealthy places, shared by a man and his wife, their children and the few farm animals they may have been fortunate enough to possess—a pig, perhaps, and a few chickens.

There were six small settlements in the West Derby hundred and a small castle was built in the town itself, probably by Roger of Poictou, where a court of justice was established. One of these settlements or "berewickes" was Liverpool. There are no records to tell us how it first came into existence, but it developed on the northern shores of the Mersey estuary, at the

The first settlement

point where a tidal creek runs inland for about half a mile, in a north-westerly direction, to enclose a small, sheltered peninsula, which is highest in the south and slopes gently down to the north.

On this peninsula, overlooking the Mersey to the south and the creek or "pool" to the east, the first inhabitants of Liverpool settled: a handful of medieval serfs, who derived most of their living from the abundant fish of the Mersey estuary, and were dependants of the manor of West Derby.

No one can say with certainty how the hamlet received its name. Liverpool may have meant the "Lower Pool" or perhaps the "Pool of the Slopes" or the "Pool of the Rushes", for "lever" was the word for a rush or flag. Again it may have been derived from the "livered pool", meaning the "pool with thick water". Although the people of Liverpool were such a small and isolated community, there was no escaping their feudal duties. They were allotted land to the north and west of their settlement, the "Old Field", between present-day Islington and Great Nelson Street, to cultivate for their own use and were allowed to graze their cattle and pigs on the commons and woodlands beyond. In return they cultivated the land of their lord. The fishermen had to pay him for a licence to fish and probably give him part of their catch, and if they sold any fish to the inland hamlets they would have needed a marketing licence.

These peasants were mainly self-supporting for their needs. They produced their own food and built their own huts. They spun and wove rough cloth for their clothing. In fact, they handled very little money, but such necessities as pots and pans, needles and thread and agricultural tools they probably bought from a visiting pedlar, who most likely came from Chester, the nearest big town; or they may sometimes have visited Chester market themselves, though it was a difficult journey, incurring the expense of the ferry boat.

Very little is known about Roger of Poictou, but it was probably he who created the great deer park around Toxteth and Smeddon—a stretch of forest covering 2,300 acres which was surrounded by a seven-mile wall. Like the royal forests of Hampshire and Windsor, this would have been subject to the hated forest laws which forbade anyone but the owners and their friends to hunt the forest animals, under penalty of severe punishment or even death. There is no doubt that if the forest animals had not been protected in this way they would have disappeared more quickly than they did, but at one time a third of England's land was enclosed for private hunting and it created a real hardship amongst the peasants, for they were deprived of a valuable source of food, particularly in winter, when they needed it most.

In 1102, by which time William's son Henry I was reigning, Roger of Poictou and his family, loyal to Robert of Normandy, with whom Henry was at war, were banished from the kingdom. The vast estate of south Lancashire was confiscated by Henry and remained in the hands of the royal family for many years to come, but when Henry II succeeded, he made a grant of the small manor of Liverpool to Warin, his chief falconer, who was Constable of Lancaster Castle.

When King John came to the throne, he confirmed this gift to Warin's son, Henry Fitzwarin, and it is in this deed that the name of Liverpool first appears. The manor at this time was cultivated by fifty-three villeins, sixty-two day labourers, three ploughmen, six herdsmen, one horseman, four bondmen and three bondwomen; so the population had changed very little since the days of the Conqueror, a hundred and thirty years earlier, and Liverpool was still an isolated, lonely little backwater.

Elsewhere in England there were many changes, for the country was beginning to prosper from the export of wool to Europe.

Most of England's foreign trade was based on the City of London, and the rest passed mainly through the ports on the south and east coasts.

From the ports, goods were carried inland by the rivers wherever possible, for there were very few roads in England and such as did exist were bad and were to remain so for centuries to come. The Anglo-Saxons had added tracks to the main Roman roads, but they were not properly surfaced and it was nobody's business to maintain them. In winter, packhorses and men floundered in the mud, while in summer the roads dried into deep, dangerous ruts.

Chester, where the Romans had built a fort to defend the Dee crossing when they advanced into North Wales, was the largest town of the north-west, and in the Domesday Book it was recorded as having five hundred houses. Here William I had established the Earldom of Chester. Chester Castle was built and became the seat of government for a long line of powerful earls, who received a large income from trade in the valuable Cheshire salt deposits. Salt was carried round the coast to other ports. It was taken up the Dee to reach inland districts. And it was transported across the Irish Sea to Ireland.

Ireland, at the time of the Norman invasion of England, was a country of mixed races: descendants of Celtic invaders from England, Gaels from Gaul, and Norsemen who had settled in the north, establishing Dublin and other small independent towns. The Gaels were the aristocrats, ruling a number of small, separate kingdoms, which were invariably at war with each other, and when Dermot, King of Leinster, saw his land threatened by Rory O'Connor of Connaught, he asked Henry II for permission to enlist the help of some of the Norman lords of the Welsh marches.

The Norman barons, with their armoured knights, men-at-arms and skilled bowmen, set sail from Bristol and Chester. Foremost among them was Richard de Clare, known as Strongbow, who very soon made himself not only Lord of Leinster, but of the independent Norse city of Dublin as well, to the fury of the citizens of Dublin and many of the other Irish kings. Henry II, more concerned that his barons might become too powerful than with the feelings of the outraged Irish, crossed to Ireland himself, to assert his authority.

He established himself as Lord of Ireland and the Irish kings throughout the country seemed content to recognize him as such, for his visit had the blessing of the Pope and the campaign was a peaceful one.

Chester prospered during these Irish journeys and the port dues filled the earl's coffers, but the little settlement of Liverpool, only a few miles to the north, remained much as it had been for the last century or more, cut off from the main stream of development which was taking place throughout the rest of the country—a lonely, desolate place, its few inhabitants hard-working, simple peasants who knew little about life outside their own hamlet.

With the gradual development of commerce and overseas trade, the people of England, particularly those living in towns and cities, grew richer and the old feudal system broke down. English merchants and shopkeepers exchanged their feudal dues and duties for payment of rent. The first trade gilds came into existence and they began to manage their own affairs.

The situation did not change so quickly in the country districts, where the bulk of the population still lived, but the more successful villeins were able to buy their freedom by exchanging their labour for payment of rent.

In Norman times many new towns were built. Some grew up round the new castles, to supply the daily wants of the castle households. Others developed from ancient market towns which had been in existence for centuries, either on the coast, round convenient harbours, or inland where tracks met or rivers could be easily forded. Still more were created by the king or wealthy landowners who were anxious to develop their estates and increase their incomes by market dues. When they founded a borough it was settled by men who were willing to rent plots of land and live there for purposes of trade. There were advantages on both sides. The landlord received rents and taxes. The tenants were relieved of all feudal duties and were free men. In time, a peasant who managed to escape from his feudal lord and had sufficient means to rent a holding or "burgage" in a town for a year and a day was entitled to call himself a free man.

Henry II set up the borough of Woodstock. Richard I gave Portsmouth its first charter. The Bishop of Worcester laid out Stratford-upon-Avon, in 1196. The Priors of Plympton founded the town of Plymouth and Richard Poore, who became Bishop of Salisbury, planned Salisbury, outside the gates of the old walled city of Sarum, along the shores of the Avon.

The inhabitants of these early towns—the weavers, tailors, drapers, the grocers and butchers, bakers, pastrycooks, vintners, brewers and innkeepers, goldsmiths, blacksmiths, pewterers, saddlers, tanners, dyers, glovers and shoemakers, bowyers and fletchers, tilers, carpenters and builders—lived a life which was, nevertheless, still very close to the countryside, and outside the town walls were the town fields, with their strips of agricultural land and the commons where they could graze their sheep and cattle.

When King John came to the throne, it was the turn of Liverpool to become a borough. John had inherited the Princedom of Ireland from his father, and news had reached him that the Norman barons were encroaching on some of the Irish kingdoms and causing trouble. He wanted to visit Ireland and

King John presents Liverpool with its charter

exert his authority over the barons, as Henry II had done. For this venture he needed a port of embarkation on the west coast. He was not on good terms with the powerful Earl of Chester, who in any case ruled the city almost as an independent prince and would have charged exorbitant port dues. John was himself the Duke of Lancaster, for Lancashire was still part of the Crown lands, but there was no developed port on the Lancashire coast. However, during a tour of the county he arrived at Liverpool, the gift of which he had confirmed, at the beginning of his reign, to Henry Fitzwarin. King John saw the sheltered pool leading into the wide Mersey estuary. As a harbour it would be even better than Chester, for the sands of the Dee, which were eventually to make Chester unusable as a port, were already beginning to choke the estuary.

He asked Henry Fitzwarin of Lancaster to exchange Liverpool for other lands. Henry could not refuse and King John became Lord of Liverpool. On 28th August, 1207, he issued an invitation to settlers to come and live in his new port of Liverpool, in return for which he would give them the privileges of inhabitants of a borough.

This open letter from the sovereign ran as follows: "John, by the Grace of God, King of England, Lord of Ireland, Duke of Normandy and Aquitaine, Earl of Anjou, To all his faithful people who would wish to have burgages at the town of Lyverpul, Greeting; Know ye that we have granted to all our faithful people who shall have taken burgages at Lyverpul, that they shall have all the liberties and free customs in the town of Lyverpul which any free borough on the sea hath in our land; and we therefore command you that ye shall securely and in our peace come there to receive and inhabit our burgages; and in testimony hereof we send you our letters patent,—Witness, S. de Pateshill, at Winchester, the 28th day of August, in the ninth year of our reign."

It was to prove the beginning of Liverpool's close association with Ireland and the Irish, and was to set the little fishing hamlet on the long road to fame and riches as a great seaport city.

2. LIVERPOOL BECOMES A TOWN

Liverpool was not yet made into a self-governing borough. Such a privilege had to be bought and the burgesses had little ready money. Nevertheless, the town was now established as a free port, a borough and a centre of trade.

The King's agents set about planning the town. It was laid out in seven streets. From north to south, in a continuous line along the crest of the ridge were the three main streets, where Old Hall Street, High Street and Castle Street now run. Two parallel streets ran from the ridge at right-angles down to the river, about where Water Street and Chapel Street now stand, and another pair, on the sites of Dale Street and Tithebarn Street, ran inland.

Along these streets a hundred and eighty plots were staked out, each with room for a long garden for vegetables and perhaps a small orchard. These plots were called burgages and the rent of each, including the tenant's right to cultivate about two acres of the town fields, was a shilling a year.

The original humble inhabitants of the little settlement of Liverpool thus became free men, and as inhabitants of burgages were known as burgesses. They were joined by families from West Derby and other nearby manors who were prepared to try their fortune in the new venture.

King John gave permission for a weekly market to be held every Saturday, where the burgesses could rent their stalls at a lower rate than visiting salesmen and did not have to pay dues for the maintenance of the market court.

At the point where Castle Street, Dale Street and Water Street met the High Cross was erected, and where Chapel Street, Tithebarn Street and Old Hall Street met, the White

Cross: round these two crosses the market stalls were set up for the sale of corn, meat, fish and other commodities.

Although life in medieval England was in many ways harsh and cruel, people had a keen sense of justice and fair play. The market courts not only established a fair rate of charges for goods but also set a standard of quality and workmanship and enforced the settlement of debts.

For those who attempted to cheat, the punishment was made to fit the crime. A vintner who sold bad wine was forced to drink some of it himself and the rest was poured over his head. A fishmonger or poulterer who sold bad produce was placed in a pillory and, with his head so firmly fixed that he could not

A baker is punished for cheating his customers

move it, the fish or bird was burnt under his nose. A baker who sold underweight loaves was made to look ridiculous by being dragged about the town on a cart, with a loaf of bread tied round his neck.

King John also granted permission for a three-day fair to be held in Liverpool each November. It was at these medieval trade fairs that most of the wholesale buying for the year was done and they were held at most of the important towns throughout the country. The famous fair at Stourbridge, near Cambridge, which had also been licensed by King John, was visited by merchants from every country in northern Europe, as well as all parts of England and Wales. It lasted for three weeks and the fairground covered a square mile.

The fair at Liverpool was very small compared with Stourbridge, but King John no doubt hoped to make the town a centre of trade for the whole of Lancashire. Most of the merchants would have had to approach the town by sea and the King, being chronically short of money, probably had an eye on their ships, hoping that he might be able to hire them sometimes for his Irish and French expeditions.

Fairs and market days were cheerful occasions and the stretch of the High Street between Castle Street and Old Hall Street was originally known as Juggler Street, for it was here that the jugglers and musicians used to assemble, to amuse the crowds.

Over the new borough of Liverpool, though it was still little more than an isolated village, a royal bailiff was appointed, to collect rents and taxes and preside over the newly established court of justice.

By 1210 King John was ready for his visit to Ireland, and while his men and ships waited at Liverpool for a fair wind to carry them across the Irish Sea the little town was kept busy supplying them with food and drink. The main purpose of the King's visit was to assert his authority over the Norman settlers, for Ireland had become a haven for rebellious barons, and their growing strength was becoming dangerous. With no bloodshed, King John and his army marched from Dublin across Ireland, southwards, westwards and then to the north. In two months he visited nearly the whole of Norman-occupied Ireland and all the Norman barons paid homage to him, swearing to conform to the laws of England; this was "but a mere mockery and imposture . . . for his back was no sooner turned but they returned to their former rebellion".

It was to be another two hundred years before an English king set foot again in Ireland and during this time, despite the appointment of a succession of English judges and governors to Dublin, the Norman colonies were left mainly to themselves, "to maintain what they had got, and to gain more if they could".

Six years after King John returned from Ireland, he was dead, and during the last troubled years of his reign life in the little port of Liverpool moved slowly and uneventfully. The royal bailiff collected the dues for the King and presided over the court of law. There were two "solemn meetings" of this Port Moot each year, which all the burgesses had to attend, but at the other meetings, called every few weeks to settle minor disputes and problems, only those burgesses directly concerned had to appear.

It was the Normans who built the first windmills and water-mills in England and at Liverpool a watermill was built in the stream which flows into the pool behind the modern art gallery. Here peasants brought their corn to be ground, paying a small fee for the services of the miller. The mill was one of the earliest labour-saving devices and a great advance on the old method of grinding corn by hand, between two heavy millstones.

For many years to come the parish church of Liverpool, where marriages and burials were solemnized, was at Walton, but it was probably during this early part of the twelfth century that the first little church of St Mary-on-the-Quay was built on the Mersey waterfront, where the churchyard of St Nicholas church stands today. St Mary-on-the-Quay was very small, consisting of a simple nave, with no aisles, and a chancel over which was built a square tower, for the population of the town was only a few hundred and during King John's reign he received only £9 a year from all the rents and taxes. Never-theless, the burgesses of Liverpool slowly prospered, mainly through trade with Ireland and the passage of troops and officials to Dublin Castle, the English citadel for the defence of the city and the seat of government for the English colony.

When John's successor, Henry III, came of age his main ambition was to recover his family's lost domains in France and, being desperate for money with which to wage the French wars, he gave the burgesses of Liverpool an opportunity to buy certain privileges for themselves. In 1229 they bought a new charter, costing £6 13s 4d, which enabled them to elect their own officers, instead of being controlled by the royal bailiff. Their own court was now given the power to deal with all matters relating to property in the borough and they no longer had to attend the Hundreds Court at West Derby. They were also given the right to form themselves into trade gilds, for which they were allowed to charge an entrance fee.

Within a week or two they obtained even more privileges. By paying £10 a year they were given the right to collect the rent of the burgages themselves, as well as the tolls paid by strangers trading in the market, the fines imposed by the Port Moot court and the profits from the mill and the newly-established ferry across the Mersey.

This meant that the royal bailiff was no longer necessary and Liverpool became an almost independent community, answerable only to the King. The borough elected its own officers, administered its own court of law, paid its rents to the community and worked the mills and the ferry for its own benefit.

This annual payment, by which a borough "bought out" the Lord, was known as a "fee farm rent". In the case of Liverpool the arrangement was made for only a limited number of years. When the lease ended a new arrangement had to be made and with each new Lord of Liverpool there were arguments and discussions about the fee farm rent and the rights of the burgesses.

Only a few months after selling Liverpool so many privileges, Henry III granted all his Lancashire lands, including Liverpool, to the Earl of Chester and three years later, when the Earl died, his property went to his brother-in-law, William de Ferrers, Earl of Derby.

Both these earls accepted the fee farm rent of the burgesses without question and between 1232 and 1237 William de Ferrers built Liverpool Castle. The site, fifty feet above sea level, was well chosen, for this was the highest point of the small triangle of land which the Pool almost enclosed, and being at the southern end of the peninsula, it controlled the harbour entrance admirably. A plateau of rock fifty feet square was first marked out. Then a defensive ditch, twenty yards

Liverpool Castle

wide, was cut round it, forming a dry moat. The fortress was
square. At the three corners of the main surrounding or
"curtain" wall three circular towers were built and near the
fourth corner a massive gate house, facing northwards on to
Castle Street, with towers on either side. A causeway over the
moat led to the portcullis, behind which was an archway giving
on to the castle courtyard, in which were built the hall, a chapel
and barracks for the garrison. The largest of the towers, at the
south-west corner, was the keep, where the lord lived when
he was in residence, and along the western wall, alongside the
river, was a banqueting hall, with kitchens, a bakehouse and a
brewery.

In this wall there was a small gate from which steps led
down to the moat, and from here a secret tunnel ran through
to the edge of the river, so that if the castle were besieged food
supplies could be brought in, or, if things became desperate,
the defenders could make their escape.

The Derby family were Lords of Liverpool for two generations but Robert de Ferrers, William's grandson, joined Simon
de Montfort's rebellion against Henry III, and when it failed he

and his family lost all their estates, which were granted to Henry's second son Edmund, who was created Earl of Derby and, the following year, Earl of Lancaster.

Edmund was by no means as popular in Liverpool as the de Ferrers had been, for he would not renew the lease of the fee farm rents. Instead he appointed his own bailiff and by 1292 had extracted £25 from the burgesses instead of the £10 they had formerly paid.

During Simon de Montfort's brief spell as head of state he had summoned two knights from every county and two citizens from every borough to attend the first English Parliament. Liverpool had not sent representatives on that occasion, but in 1295 and again in 1307 was called upon to send two members to Westminster. From the remote parts of the country the journey to Westminster was difficult, dangerous and expensive, and many boroughs ignored the summons, so that, for many years to come, the Parliamentary system did not work effectively. It was only after communications and transport improved that it became practical, and after 1307 it was to be another two hundred years before Liverpool was again represented at Westminster.

In 1295 Edmund died and his son Thomas succeeded to the Earldom of Lancaster. In 1307 Edward I died and the disastrous reign of the unfortunate Edward II began. In 1314 his army was routed by Robert Bruce at the battle of Bannockburn and for years to come Scottish troops ravaged the border country as far south as Lancashire. In Ireland, Robert Bruce's brother, Edward, landed in 1315, announcing that he had come to deliver Ireland from the English, and at first he had such success that he fomented a rebellion amongst the Irish and was actually proclaimed King of Ireland. The English barons in Ireland united to quell the Irish and drive out the Scots, but needed reinforcements from England, most of which passed through Liverpool, before Edward Bruce was finally defeated and killed, at the end of 1318.

In England, the barons, led by Thomas, Earl of Lancaster, rebelled against the ineptitude of Edward II's rule. In 1322

Earl Thomas was captured at the battle of Boroughbridge, tried by court martial at his own castle of Pontefract and immediately beheaded. The following year, Edward II paid a visit to Liverpool and stayed for a week in the castle. Four years later he was deposed and shortly afterwards murdered. With the accession of Edward III, Thomas's heir, his brother Henry was reinstated as Earl of Lancaster, but there was still no peace. Shortly after his accession, Edward III began the disastrous war with France which dragged on for the next century and was known as the Hundred Years War. Though the southern ports were mainly used for the embarkation of troops for France, Liverpool was still kept busy with the passage of troops and supplies to Scotland and Ireland.

In the middle of the fourteenth century disaster came to Europe with the spread of the bubonic plague, known as the Black Death. It was first brought from China by Italian sailors who landed at Genoa; it then spread through Italy and southern France, and thence to Spain and England, where the first signs occurred in the west country early in 1348. By the autumn the Black Death had reached London and at its worst period two thousand Londoners were dying each day. As it moved north Liverpool suffered badly. So many died that it was impossible to carry the dead for burial to the parish church at Walton and the burgesses had to obtain a licence from the Bishop of Lichfield for the churchyard of St Mary-on-the-Quay to be used for a burial ground. By the beginning of 1349 the plague had broken out in Ireland and no one can say what havoc it wrought. The disease was most deadly among the undernourished and most of the Irish were desperately poor, but there are no records of the thousands who must have died.

In Europe 25 million people perished by the Black Death before it had spent itself, and in England, between 1348 and 1351, more than one-third of the entire population died, amounting to a million men, women and children.

However, Liverpool, along with the rest of the country, slowly recovered. The fighting continued in France. Border warfare between England and Scotland was as savage as ever and in Ireland conditions grew steadily worse as the Irish waged bitter war against the English colony around Dublin.

On two occasions the Viceroy of Ireland and his armies passed through Liverpool and more than once all shipping in the west country was ordered to assemble in the Mersey for the transport of troops to Ireland.

Towards the end of the century, Edward III's son, John of Gaunt, became Duke of Lancaster, and under his lordship the citizens of Liverpool regained all their former rights and privileges. Now that the lord's power over the town had almost gone, his bailiff was no longer necessary, so the town elected their own major bailiff, who came to be known as the Major or Mayor, under whom worked two bailiffs, one elected by the burgesses and the other chosen by the Mayor himself.

The first recorded Mayor of Liverpool was William, son of Adam of Liverpool, who took office in 1351. The Liverpool family had risen to great eminence and prosperity in the borough and owned fifteen burgages. William served Liverpool well and held office eleven times. He helped to build the new church of St Nicholas alongside the little St Mary-on-the-

Ancient chapel of Toxteth which was later built in Toxteth Park

Quay, for by this time St Mary's was too small for the growing community, which had increased to about a thousand.

William was a miller and also owned a bakery in Castle Street and a fishery near Toxteth Park. The old watermill had been replaced by two windmills—the Eastham mill, near the old watermill, and the Town End mill, on the site of the present Wellington column opposite St George's Hall.

The Liverpools owned the Eastham mill, and the Town End mill belonged to a rival family, the Moores, who had a good deal of land in Liverpool as well as large estates in the surrounding country. Their original home was the Old Hall, where Old Hall Street now stands, which they left when they built Bank Hall, at Kirkdale.

Both families were anxious to control the government of Liverpool, but while William of Liverpool was Mayor no Moore held office. When he died, in 1383, Thomas Moore became Mayor and his family was powerful in the administration of the town for many years to come.

William of Liverpool's land and mill passed through marriage to the Crosse family, who also were to become distinguished in their service to the borough. They lived at Crosse Hall, where Crosshall Street now runs, off Dale Street.

The castle does not appear to have played much part in the life of Liverpool in the later years of the fourteenth century. It was governed by a constable, who was also Ranger of Toxteth Park, but he was not often in residence, and when he did stay in Liverpool it was usually in a small house near the gates, outside the castle precincts. The castle was used occasionally for a prison, although it was equipped to house a small garrison of soldiers if the necessity should arise. An inventory at this time included 186 pallet beds, 107 spears, 39 lances, 15 catapults for hurling stones and a few siege engines, all of which were in the charge of a watchman and a doorkeeper, who were paid a halfpenny a day each.

With the beginning of the fifteenth century there were many changes in the social and commercial life of England as a whole and many parts of the country began to prosper from the wool-weaving industry, which was growing steadily in importance. Liverpool, however, did not share in this prosperity and was to suffer grievously during the Wars of the Roses, which followed on the ignominious end of the Hundred Years War.

Two important noble families arrived in the town at this time. Sir John Stanley from Cheshire had married the daughter of Sir Thomas Lathom and thereby acquired, amongst many other possessions, some land in Liverpool. In 1403, as a reward for his valour at the battle of Shrewsbury, he had been granted the Isle of Man, and the Stanley family remained Kings of the Island, answerable only to the monarchs of England, until 1737.

Sir John decided to build a stronghold for himself in Liverpool, which would serve as a base for men and supplies for his new kingdom, and obtained permission to fortify and enlarge an old stone house which stood on the riverside at the bottom of Water Street. This was the Liverpool Tower, which remained until 1819.

In 1441, during the reign of Henry VI, Sir Richard Molyneux, whose family were long-standing enemies of the Stanleys, was made Constable of Liverpool Castle, and this office was made hereditary to his family. Sir Richard took up residence in the castle and the following year built a new tower in the south-east corner, which was of alarming and threatening strength. So the burgesses of Liverpool, in their small, defenceless timbered cottages, found themselves with two powerful families, at daggers-drawn, entrenched in fortified strongholds in their very midst.

When the Wars of the Roses broke out, both the Molyneux family and the Stanleys declared for the Yorkists, but Liverpool was in the heart of the Lancastrian country. There are no records left of what exactly happened in Liverpool during these years of anarchy and savage bloodshed, but while the kings and princes of medieval England worked out their violent destinies, the burgesses must have been the helpless victims of untold suffering and distress.

At the end of it all, they were so impoverished that they

were unable to pay the fee farm rent which the King's bailiff now demanded. It was reduced from £25 to £23, then to £14 and finally to £11, which was only £2 more than King John had received, more than two hundred and fifty years earlier.

3. LIVERPOOL IN TUDOR TIMES

With the accession of Henry VII the bitter feuds and wars between the barons and princes, which had ravaged the country for so long, came to an end. England was still an agricultural country, with a population of less than four million, but with relative peace for a few years she was able to develop her overseas trade and her industries, the most important of which were the spinning of wool and the weaving of woollen cloth. The spinning wheel replaced the old hand-spindle and distaff about this time, and men and women wove the cloth in their own cottages, on small hand-looms.

For many years Liverpool did not share in this prosperity, although Manchester was already becoming a busy centre of the weaving industry. Leland, the historian, wrote in 1533 that the town was "well set a-work in making of clothes as well of linen as of woollen". The flax for the linen came from Ireland, through Liverpool and Chester, but the main market for Manchester's exports was Europe, so that her manufactured goods were sent to the east coast ports or by pack-horse train to London.

During the previous century Liverpool's small trade had been almost entirely with Ireland, her ships carrying rough, woollen cloth from Lancashire and Yorkshire, iron from Furness and salt from Cheshire and returning with hides, flax and wool. Only very rarely did a Liverpool ship trade as far as France, bringing back French wine.

The only manufactures in the little port were to supply local needs and amongst its thousand inhabitants there were three weavers, four drapers, two tailors, one bow-maker, one tanner, four bootmakers, five leather workers, five fish merchants and two blacksmiths, while nearly every household manufactured its own beer. Although there were a few prosperous burgesses, notably the Crosse family and the Moores, most of the people were poor, many renting only half a burgage, from which they obtained enough produce on which to live, while by this time there were also people, such as servants and labourers, who owned nothing and did not possess the privileges of the burgesses. When bad times came, therefore, through illness, accident or unemployment, they had no reserves and were soon destitute. In time people who were not burgesses but nevertheless prospered were able to buy burgess privileges. They were known as free men and the term "freeman" eventually came to be used in place of "burgess".

The Irish trade declined, for conditions in Ireland were chaotic. To add to Liverpool's troubles, the town was stricken by a fresh outbreak of plague. A third of her people died and by 1565 the population was down to only 700.

About this time, Liverpool seamen owned between them thirteen vessels, employing two hundred men, but the largest ship was only 100 tons; forty years later the number of ships had risen to only twenty. Yet these were the days of the great sea journeys of Christopher Columbus and John Cabot to the New World and the first visits of English merchant ships to the Guinea coast of Africa.

As Mary Tudor was married to Philip of Spain, English seamen did not pay much attention to the New World at first, leaving it to the Spaniards and Portuguese. After Queen Mary's death, Philip remained friendly with Queen Elizabeth for some years, so the Spaniards still had no rivals in the Americas. Both the Spaniards and the Portuguese had begun to use Negro slave labour for their plantations and mines in the New World and as early as 1562 Sir John Hawkins undertook to carry slaves for Spain from West Africa to America, a practice of which Queen Elizabeth strongly disapproved.

It was during the 1570s and 1580s, when the friendship with Spain was rapidly cooling, that England began to show her naval supremacy and entered the race for the treasures of the

New World and the discovery of even newer lands and markets.

In 1577 Francis Drake sailed from Plymouth and during three years of incredible hardships sailed right round the world. Three years later Sir Humphrey Gilbert took possession of Newfoundland, in the name of Queen Elizabeth. His half-brother, Sir Walter Raleigh, led an expedition to North America and staked a claim for England which he called Virginia. By 1585 the first colonists settled there, under the leadership of Sir Walter's cousin, Sir Richard Grenville. That colony was a failure and they were all brought back to England, but it proved a useful experiment for future settlements.

By 1588, the year of the Armada, Queen Elizabeth granted a patent for the Guinea trade to a new company of merchant adventurers, in open defiance of Portugal, at that time Spain's close ally, who claimed a monopoly of the African trade.

Yet aside from a little piracy in the Irish sea against Spanish ships, Liverpool, small and poor, took no part. During the troubles of the fifteenth century she had lost the right to collect the royal dues of the borough and with the advent of the Tudors she was involved in constant arguments with the royal bailiffs about the fee farm rents. In time, however, a few compensations came her way. She acquired possession of the waste land between the borough and Toxteth Park which, in the years to come, was to prove a valuable asset. It had originally been leased to the town by John of Gaunt, but by long usage it gradually came to be accepted as the borough's property.

In 1516 John Crosse, a member of the Crosse Hall family who had entered the Church and was living in London, bequeathed all his property in Liverpool for a chantry. This meant that the income from the property went towards paying a priest to pray for his soul and the souls of his family and also keep a grammar school, at which all poor boys of Liverpool and boys of the name of Crosse were to receive a free education. The fees of other scholars were to go towards the salary of a teacher, and he and the priest were to be appointed by the Mayor and certain members of the Crosse family. John Crosse also presented a house to the borough in which the court and other borough business could be conducted. This was Liverpool's first Town Hall, a small, thatched building which stood in the High Street, while the grammar school, so called because the principal subject taught was Latin grammar, was held in St Nicholas church.

Only a few years after its foundation, Henry VIII's Reformation meant the end of the chantries. Many chantry schools disappeared, though most, including the John Crosse school, were soon reorganized as Protestant foundations.

It is difficult to tell how deeply the people of Liverpool were affected by the Reformation. Materially it made little difference and although so many Lancashire families suffered persecution for their loyalty to the Pope, in Liverpool the people seemed to accept the Anglican Church with little difficulty. With the passing years they became staunch Protestants and towards the end of the century many were Puritans.

By 1545 the borough was represented in Parliament again, by two members, but they were nominated by the Chancellor of the Duchy of Lancaster and the Earl of Derby and were not Liverpool men. In 1568, for example, Francis Bacon was a member for Liverpool, but there is no record that he ever even visited the town. On one occasion, in 1563, when Liverpool flouted the Chancellor and sent its own member to Westminster, at its own expense, the full force of the Chancellor's fury was only averted by the timely intervention of the Earl of Derby, the "patron and good friend" of Liverpool.

Towards the end of the century, the old medieval government of the borough, with its general assembly of burgesses and freemen, who could always outvote the decisions of the Mayor and aldermen, was simplified, and the town was governed by a council composed of twenty-four ordinary citizens and twelve aldermen, who were men who had held office as Mayor. This council was elected for life and led by an annually-appointed Mayor. The arrangement was less democratic but more efficient, and this was the construction of the council which ruled Liverpool until the Municipal Reform Act of 1835.

The prosperity of Chester, like that of Liverpool, had declined, partly through an outbreak of the plague and also because of a fall in the Irish trade. It was the renewal of the Irish rebellions and the Tudor determination to try to settle them that made Chester and Liverpool busy again. Trouble had flared up in Ireland when the full effect of the Reformation made itself felt. In 1549 the English Book of Common Prayer was introduced, but very few obeyed the order to use it, and when French and Spanish envoys and Roman Catholic missionaries arrived in the country Irish opposition stiffened. Things quietened down during Catholic Mary's short reign, but when Queen Elizabeth came to the throne matters grew steadily worse, for both the native Irish and the long-established Anglo-Irish, many of whom had married into Irish families by now, were devout Roman Catholics, as well as most of the English colony who were now living within the "Pale", a fortified double ditch which had been dug round their territory, centred on Dublin.

The English of the Pale remained loyal to England, but elsewhere Irish and Anglo-Irish united and in 1569 rebellion broke out. They were supported by the Pope and, as relations between England and Spain deteriorated to the verge of war, Philip also promised help.

Bitter fighting continued for the next fourteen years, until 1583, by which time much of Munster had been reduced to utter desolation and its population cruelly ravaged by famine and disease. With the final outbreak of war with Spain and the defeat of the Armada in 1588, the English government decided to repopulate Munster with loyal families. Four million acres of land were confiscated and divided into estates varying in size from 4,000 to 12,000 acres. These were granted to English "undertakers", who agreed to sub-let them to English-born tenants. Four years later, only thirteen of the fifty-eight "undertakers" were living in Ireland and only 245 families had been installed from England. Many undertakers had let their lands to Irish families and others had sold them back to their original owners.

There was no profit to be made from the ravaged land of Munster and the scheme failed, leaving the Irish more resentful than ever. By the following year trouble flared up in Ulster, led by O'Neill, Earl of Tyrone, which quickly spread to Connaught and Leinster. The Munster settlements were destroyed and an English army 20,000 strong was despatched by way of Chester and Liverpool, under the command of the Earl of Essex. As a commander, the Earl was a failure. He was recalled to England, tried and executed; and his command in Ireland was given to Lord Mountjoy. The next year a Spanish fleet landed 4,000 men at Kinsale, but before O'Neill could join them, Lord Mountjoy's army attacked. The Spaniards surrendered and were allowed to return to Spain. O'Neill fled back to Ulster. Elsewhere in Ireland the rebellion had faded away and he had few allies left, but he was not captured until 1603, six days after the death of Queen Elizabeth.

At the beginning of these wars Chester played a more important part than Liverpool in the transport of troops and equipment, for she had more ships at her disposal. She fought hard to keep this lead and insisted that the Mersey was only a creek of the port of Chester and that all ships using it should pay customs and dues to Chester. The Liverpool men protested vigorously and eventually threatened a legal battle before their independence was accepted.

It was a disaster beyond the control of Chester which at last brought about the decline of the port. The shifting sands of the Dee were moving again and making navigation increasingly difficult. By 1597 the Lord Deputy of Ireland, in a request for more equipment for Dublin, wrote that it would reach him more quickly from Liverpool, "for that the conveniency of shipping commonly serveth at Liverpool rather than at Chester".

Chester as a port was by no means dead, but from this time onwards Liverpool drew ahead in usefulness and importance.

Yet Liverpool by the end of the sixteenth century was still very small and had changed hardly at all in two hundred years. The burgages of the original streets were still surrounded by fields and most of the population lived as their forefathers had done, by agriculture. The Earl of Derby was not often in residence at the tower nor the Molyneux family at the castle.

A few merchants traded as far as Spain and Portugal, taking out corn and rough woollen cloth and returning with wine and Spanish iron, but mainly the trade was with Ireland, when the troubles permitted. Flax for the handlooms of Manchester and hides and sheepskins for the tanners of Liverpool were imported and in exchange went linen from Manchester and Kendal, woollens from Yorkshire, coal from Wigan, knives and agricultural implements from Sheffield, pewter from Chester, bridles and saddles which had probably been made in Liverpool; but one interesting cargo, in 1586, included 1,400 tennis balls and 240 rackets.

In this rather desolate and isolated little port life was extraordinarily well organized. While the soldiers were being transported to Ireland there are records of street fighting and drunken brawls, but the town made a profit from the army, for it cost two shillings and sixpence to transport each soldier and two shillings was allowed to each man for food on the journey, and while the armies waited in Liverpool for a sailing they were allowed threepence for each meal and fourpence a day for the feed of every horse.

Commerce was strictly controlled. A ship's master had to pay anchorage and wharfage when he arrived in Liverpool and then had to interview the Mayor to arrange the terms on which he would sell the cargo. If he chose a "town bargain" his cargo was valued by town officials, called "prysors". The town then collected customs duties and the goods were taken to the cellar under the town hall, where every freeman had the right to buy them at the price decreed by the prysors. If the merchant decided to sell his cargo on his own terms, he had to buy a licence, and even then only freemen were allowed to buy them, the rest of the community having to buy second-hand from the freemen.

The Saturday market was also beset by rules and regulations. Space was allotted for each commodity. Lancashire men had to sell their corn on the east side of the street, for example, and Cheshire men on the west. Before the market opened, the Mayor and his officers inspected all the goods for sale and checked the weights and measures against the town standards; and for the first hour, only freemen were allowed to buy.

During the three days of the fair, when merchants came from far afield, the ritual was even more complicated. The boundary of the fairground was clearly marked and once they were safely inside it debtors were immune from arrest while the fair lasted. To this day, the "liberty stone" still stands in Castle Street.

Milling was the most important industry of the town and people still had to use the services of the millers at the Eastham and Town End mills. Anyone who tried to assert his independence and build his own hand or horse mill ran the risk of having it destroyed, for private mills were regarded as illegal.

Brewing was strictly supervised and two officers were appointed each year to inspect all beer that was sold and ensure that it was of good quality and fair measure.

By 1573 a set of stocks had been put up at the High Cross for the punishment of wrongdoers; a few years later, as it was

Ordeal in the stocks

proving inconvenient to house prisoners in the town hall, a house near the shore was made into a gaol. Even beggars had to have a licence to beg, but a poor house was provided to accommodate the destitute.

The borough controlled all matters concerning St Nicholas church and chose the parson. His salary was £10 a year and the borough officials kept a careful watch on his behaviour, not hesitating to dismiss him if he did not please them. One was fined "for suffering the churchyard to be spoiled with swine". Another was told "to cut his hair of a comely and seemly length, as best beseemeth a man in his place".

Yet with all these restrictions, which the people of Liverpool no doubt often ignored, they found plenty of ways of amusing themselves. Cock-fighting and bull-baiting were favourite sports and the town provided its own cock-pit. Horse-racing was popular and the borough organized a race each year on Ascension Day for a silver bell. The first race was run by four horses over a four and a half mile course on the Kirkdale sands. The town also employed a musician, who played his bagpipes morning and evening in the market place and every day before the Mayor's house and the homes of all the aldermen.

Nearly every important occasion was made the excuse for a banquet at the town hall and during the fair there was a great feast to which all freemen were invited. Many wedding feasts took place at the town hall, too, and when freemen were elected they celebrated by dispensing free beer to all comers.

Sometimes the neighbouring lords would send in food for a feast. In 1562, for example, my Lord Derby "gave the town a buck, a pure good one, and merrily disposed of and eaten in the common hall. . . . Also Sir Richard Molyneux gave the town a buck, which proved but mean, and that was divided between the Mayor, the aldermen, and the bailiffs, whereat many of the commoners loured and something murmured."

4. BESIEGED!

At the opening of the seventeenth century, England was a country of sharp contrasts. This was still the land of Shakespeare and the poets, of boisterous tavern revelry, of merrymaking and junketings on Mayday, at harvest time and hallowe'en, of hunting and hawking, journeys to strange lands and adventures on the high seas. It was also a time of intrigue, cruelty, violence and religious persecution. Amongst the ordinary people, however, there was spreading a new spirit of independence. They were better educated and many were now reading the Bible for themselves, for by this time a copy was to be found in every village and town. Men began to reshape their lives according to its doctrines and live more soberly. Many kept Sunday as a day apart, frowning upon Sunday sports and pastimes, and permitting no labour to disturb a day devoted to prayer and worship. They disagreed with even the simplified ritual of the Church of England, asserting that the sacrament should be administered "without any tradition or invention of man".

These people were the Puritans and, like the Roman Catholics, many were persecuted, fined and imprisoned for not conforming to the established Church. It did not deter them and Puritanism became especially strong in East Anglia and the Midlands, including Manchester and Liverpool.

When James I came to the throne, in 1603, both Puritans and Roman Catholics petitioned him for freedom to worship as they wished. When this was refused, the Catholics planned a rebellion, which failed at the outset with the discovery of Guy Fawkes' plot to blow up the Houses of Parliament. The Catholics were politically dangerous, because of their friend-

ship with Spain, but the Puritans were a different case. Parla-
ment pleaded for them with the King, in vain, and this was one
of the major causes of the quarrel between King and Parla-
ment which was to last for the next forty years.

"Your Majesty would be misinformed if any man should
deliver that the Kings of England have any absolute power in
themselves either to alter religion, or to make any laws concerning the same, otherwise than as in temporal causes, by
consent of Parliament," said the government to King James;
but he would yield nothing.

Early in his reign a second and more successful colony of 105
men and women, under the leadership of John Smith, was
founded in Virginia. In 1620 a group of fourteen families of
Puritans, calling themselves Independents and later known as
the Pilgrim Fathers, set sail for Massachusetts, under the leadership of John Robinson.

Five years later, Charles I succeeded his father, and, for all
his grace and charm, he proved himself as autocratic in his
dealings with Parliament as James I had been. In 1634, Lord
Baltimore, a Roman Catholic convert, founded a colony to the
north of Virginia, which he called Maryland, after Charles'
Queen, Henrietta Maria.

In Ireland, with the capture and death of O'Neill, in 1603,
there was relative peace for the next forty years and the country
made a rapid recovery, particularly during the 1620s and 1630s.
King James established English law throughout all Ireland and
the entire country was ruled from Dublin, but there were no
religious or language restrictions. The Irish remained Roman
Catholics and Gaelic was still spoken. Irish trade with Liverpool
increased and there was a steady flow through the port of Irish
flax to Manchester and Manchester-made linen back to Ireland.
Manchester was also buying cotton in London, known as
"cotton wool", which was imported by London merchants
from Cyprus and Smyrna and carried by trains of pack-horses
to Manchester for manufacture.

Most of the Irish trade went through Dublin, the bulk being
carried by English vessels, of which an increasing number came

from Liverpool compared with Chester. Liverpool also had a small trade with France and Spain but played no part yet in trade beyond Europe; though from London at this time the great sailing ships of the East India Company were making their long journeys to India and the Far East, the Levant Company was trading in the Mediterranean and the "Company of Adventurers of London Trading in Africa" had been given the exclusive rights of the Guinea trade, where competition with French, Dutch and Portuguese merchantmen had become a fight to the death. The Portuguese were offering a hundred crowns for every Frenchman's head and the Dutch were prepared to fight all comers.

Most of the developing tobacco trade with the West Indies was in the hands of the merchants of Bristol and only one shipment to Liverpool is recorded during the first half of the century.

Yet Liverpool men had their full share of violence and adventure, for the Irish Sea was as full of pirates as the Mediterranean and the African coast. In 1633, for example, a "Biscayan Spanish rogue" hovering round Dublin Bay captured two Liverpool ships, one with a cargo worth £3,000, the other carrying the Lord Deputy's own linen.

The Irish chieftains had been regranted their lands under English law by James I. The head of the O'Neill family was now known as the Earl of Tyrone and the O'Donnell chief as the Earl of Tyrconnel. Yet the English government was still suspicious of Tyrone and Tyrconnel; when the Earls learnt that their movements were being closely watched by the English Secret Service, they took alarm and, in 1607, fled into exile. This "Flight of the Earls", which for many years to come was lamented in Irish song and poetry, marked the passing of the power of the old Gaelic chieftains.

About half a million acres of their lands in Ulster were divided into new plantations, which were mostly taken by farmers from Yorkshire and Scotland, and amongst the Scots were many Presbyterians, fleeing from persecution, so that Ulster now became a stronghold of Protestantism.

Liverpool benefited, for she now received the Ulster trade as well as an increasing coastal trade, particularly with Scotland, but Catholic Ireland resented the arrival of the Protestants. Bitter quarrels flared up which were never forgiven and have been the cause of the deep unhappiness in Ireland ever since, up till the violence and bloodshed of 1970.

Ships were still very small, the average Liverpool merchantman being of about thirty tons. There were many shipwrecks, but Dublin harbour had only six feet of water at low tide and the Pool at Liverpool was not much deeper. Until the eighteenth century it was nothing more than a muddy, shallow inlet, dangerous for any ship of more than about fifty tons and quite impossible for the hundred-ton warships of the Royal Navy.

Chester still tried to claim a control over Liverpool shipping, although early in the seventeenth century she had to admit that she had no ships left and her trading was only in small barks, so that Liverpool inevitably came to be recognized as the northern port for Ireland.

Liverpool was still only a very small community and its population by the middle of the seventeenth century had risen to perhaps 1,500 or 2,000, but the Mayor and Council governed it strictly, so that the lives of the people and their trade and industry were in many ways as rigidly controlled as in medieval times. The freemen elected at least one of their two members of Parliament and amongst the officers appointed to look after the little port were the Town Clerk who, because of the various incidental fees and profits he was able to acquire, actually bought his office and grew rich, so that he was able to present the Mayor and the town with gifts of magnificent silver plate. There were four merchants who acted as Prysors, a Recorder, and a Churchwarden, who had to see that everyone went to church on Sundays and report anyone seen drinking in a tavern during service time or otherwise playing truant. There were Stewards who looked after the furniture in the Town Hall. Registers of tanned leather saw that leather was properly tanned before being offered for sale. Leavelookers examined all the food for

sale, to ensure that it was wholesome and sold nowhere but in
the market. The Town-customer and Sub-customer collected
all the dues and passed them on to the Mayor. The Hall Keeper
looked after the goods stored in the warehouse at the Town
Hall and handed them back to the owners when duties had been
paid. The Mosse Reeves and Barlimen looked after the town
boundaries and common land and prevented any encroach-
ments. The Scavengers kept the streets clean. The Hayward
looked after the town field and fences, impounded any cattle
found straying in the corn and stopped people from helping
themselves to other people's crops. The Alefounder checked the
quality and price of beer and also of bread.

In 1604 Sir Richard Molyneux released the deer park at
Toxteth from the forest laws and divided it into twenty small
farms, which were mainly tenanted by people from Bolton,
who were fervent Puritans. Still enclosed by the ancient walls
of the park, this little community lived a secluded life in what
was nicknamed the "Holy Land". In 1611 they invited Richard
Mather, a young man from Warrington, to be schoolmaster to
their children, and built him a school house in the middle of
the park. After a time he went to Oxford, but he returned in
1618 to Toxteth, as their minister as well as schoolmaster. The
farmers built a little chapel for him, which was later rebuilt
as the Ancient Chapel of Toxteth, the centre of Puritanism in
the Liverpool district.

The Mayor and Council of Liverpool still had control of St
Nicholas church, appointing the vicar and paying his salary,
and by 1629, to counteract the growing strength of Roman
Catholicism in other parts of the county, they sought permission from the bishop of the diocese for a preacher to give them
two extra sermons each month on weekdays.

They also governed John Crosse's grammar school and
appointed the schoolmaster.

Moreover, they saw to it that people behaved themselves or
paid the penalty. "Scolders and chiders" who were a nuisance
to their neighbours were fined ten shillings or imprisoned for
ten days, during which time they were allowed no wine, beer

or ale to be brought to them by sympathetic friends. In 1611, when Edward Moore was Mayor, we read in the Council Records of two men being fined for allowing their pigs to run loose on market day, on which occasion they destroyed some sacks and were a general nuisance. That year the court made an order that any servant or apprentice who was out of doors after nine o'clock, not on his master's business, was to be fined twelve pence or imprisoned.

The following year people were fined for such misdemeanours as brawling, housing a woman who had been banished from the town for petty larceny, giving shelter to someone for whom a "hue and cry" had been raised, and building a chimney so low "that it might endanger the whole town with fire".

At the end of that year, the Council decided that ten barrels of beef that had been in the warehouse unclaimed for two years should, not before time, be viewed by the merchant prysors and disposed of at the Mayor's pleasure; and in order to restrain the prysors from putting too high a value on goods, because of the percentage of tax which would go into their own pockets, it was decreed that if they were not sold because the price was too high, the prysors themselves must buy them, at the price they had fixed, another splendid example of the punishment fitting the crime.

Etiquette in church was strict. Men and women sat on opposite sides of the church and the wife of the Mayor sat in the front pew on her side, with the aldermen's wives beside her, in order of seniority. In 1614 an argument arose between Mrs Darbie and Mrs Seacombe. Mrs Darbie was the widow of an alderman who had been Mayor in 1598, and although she had remarried she claimed precedence over Mrs Seacombe, whose husband had been Mayor in 1602. She won her point, but only after hours of heated debate amongst the Councillors.

Within the next year came the case of three women who received stolen malt. They were sentenced to sit in the stocks at the High Cross on market day and were forbidden ever again to brew or sell ale. Anyone who accused the Mayor of being unjust and failed to prove his case before the Council could lose his freedom. Still more frustrating, people who even swore at the Mayor or any of the councillors, either because they had a grievance or were feeling bad-tempered, were brought to heel with a fine.

Whenever there was a funeral, a member from every household in the street had to follow the hearse to church or pay a fine of sixpence.

The Mayor was kept busy hearing all these cases; he attended his court every day from nine to eleven in the morning and from one to four in the afternoon, the aldermen joining him when they could.

By 1618 the sexton was instructed to ring a curfew at eight o'clock each evening and four o'clock each morning, and by 1629 a bellman or town crier was appointed, to broadcast the news at ten o'clock each night and four o'clock each morning, which seem extraordinarily inconvenient times. A few months later the office of beadle was created, his job being to look after any beggars who arrived in the town seeking work or shelter.

During these years one of Liverpool's famous citizens was growing to manhood—Jeremiah Horrox. He was born in 1618, at one of the farmhouses at Toxteth, and he was taught as a child by Richard Mather, who quickly discovered that his small pupil was a mathematical genius. When he was fourteen, Jeremiah went to Cambridge, studying both mathematics and astronomy.

The science of mathematics was developing rapidly and new methods were coming into use, such as logarithms and the decimal system, but it was in the field of astronomy that Jeremiah Horrox found lasting fame.

As he was completing his course at Cambridge, Richard Mather, who was an ardent Puritan and disliked Archbishop Laud's reforming zeal in the Church of England, fled to America and Jeremiah was recalled to Toxteth to take his place as preacher and teacher. In 1639, when he was still only twenty-one, he left Toxteth to become curate of Hoole, near Preston, and here, watching the stars with apparatus which he made himself, and applying his mathematics to trace their courses, he was able to calculate to the precise moment when the orbit of Venus would cross the face of the sun. Shortly afterwards he became ill. He returned to Toxteth but the following year, at the age of twenty-three, he died. Sir Isaac Newton, who was born the following year, was to describe Jeremiah Horrox, young as he was, as one of the few important English pioneers of the science of astronomy.

1641, the year of Jeremiah's death, was also the year of fresh disaster in Ireland, for rebellion broke out more terrible than ever before.

"On Saturday, the 23rd October," wrote David Macpherson, "broke out the dreadful rebellion and general defection of the Irish, and even of most of the old English papists in Ireland, who by a general massacre attempted to extirpate the whole race of protestants, and in the first three months destroyed 154,000 protestants with great cruelty, the design not being discovered till the night before.

"The Irish papists had lived quietly ever since Tyrone's rebellion was suppressed at the close of Queen Elizabeth's reign; but in the beginning of this year they had formed the execrable plot of cutting the throats of all the English. . . .

"We just briefly mention this horrid massacre," he adds unemotionally, "purely as it had a bad influence on commerce. . . ."

Liverpool's trade was, indeed, ruined for a time and a flood of Protestant refugees from Ireland arrived in the town.

King Charles' troubles were mounting rapidly. In 1634, being hard pressed for money, he had, at the instigation of Wentworth and Laud, tried to revive an ancient tax, known as Ship-money, in order to provide himself with a regular source of income. Before the establishment of a permanent English navy, the port towns had been obliged to furnish ships or their equivalent in money for the king's service. King Charles now tried to impose this tax on the whole of the country, and when John Hampden made his famous protest, thousands supported him. In Liverpool there were bitter arguments. Many refused to pay, threatening to sue the bailiffs if they attempted to extract an illegal tax, and the Council promptly passed a resolution that the cost of defending any such action should be met by the town. Eventually people were told that if they refused to pay they would lose their privileges as freemen.

While the country waited for the result of John Hampden's protest, the King insisted on the introduction of the English prayer book in the Scottish Church. The Scots refused to use it and rebellion developed into warfare. Scottish troops crossed the Tweed and occupied Northumberland and Durham and another force landed in Ireland. Charles, who had tried to dispense with Parliament, was now obliged to summon it, in order to raise money for the Scottish war. Parliament first demanded the death of Strafford and Laud and then passed a bill decreeing that they should not be dissolved again except by their own consent. For a time there was deadlock. The Puritan members of Parliament urged that the King be arrested, but others demurred, for even the moderate Anglicans feared for their religious liberties if the more fanatical Puritans gained power.

The two points of view were irreconcilable and tension mounted throughout the country. The Parliamentary party was strong in London and the counties of the south-east, where landowners had a close connection with London commerce, in East Anglia, a stronghold of Puritanism, and in most of the ports and manufacturing towns, including Liverpool and Manchester. The King drew his support from the landed gentry and yeomen farmers of the conservative, rural areas of the north, the Midlands and the west, most of whom were Anglicans, though they were joined by the Roman Catholics, of which there were still a great many in England, particularly in Lancashire and the northern counties.

By the beginning of 1642 most people realized that civil war was inevitable. In Liverpool, the Council had already ordered all aldermen and senior civic officers to have a musket and pike ready for use in their homes. All burgesses were to equip themselves with a halberd and head-piece and all freemen with a bow and arrows.

Yet Liverpool was in a difficult position. The chief local family, the Moores, were Puritans, and John Moore was their Member of Parliament, but otherwise the families of West Lancashire were staunchly Royalist. The Derby family, with their strongly fortified Liverpool Tower, were among the King's most loyal supporters, and Lathom House, their principal seat near Ormskirk, was to become a Cavalier stronghold, while the Molyneux family were Roman Catholic.

Lord Derby was a dying man, but his son, Lord Strange, shortly to succeed him, raised an army of 3,000 from the Derby tenants and seized Wigan, Preston, Lancaster and Warrington. By January, 1642, he had put a strong garrison into Liverpool and the Mayor, who had always been on good terms with the Derbys, was in no position to resist. The King set up his standard at Nottingham and war was declared, but for the next twelve months life continued uneventfully in Liverpool, under a Royalist governor whose powers superseded those of the Mayor.

The King moved from Nottingham to Shrewsbury, hoping to march on Oxford and London, but in October, 1642, he was intercepted at Edgehill, near Warwick, where the first important battle of the war was fought. Prince Rupert, the King's nephew, led his cavalry brilliantly, but the ultimate result of Edgehill was indecisive. The King proceeded to Oxford and summoned help from the new Lord Derby, who sent the bulk of his forces south for the King's service, leaving a remnant of 1,600 men, under the command of Colonel Tyldesley, to defend West Lancashire and himself hurried to the Isle of Man, where fresh troubles were brewing.

Parliamentary armies in Lancashire began a steady advance from Manchester and Colonel Tyldesley was forced to retreat to Liverpool Castle. News reached him that a Parliamentary ship was blocking the entrance to the Mersey, so there could be no escape by sea. He and his men were trapped.

The Roundhead army reached Liverpool, but the Royalists fought bitterly for two days before admitting defeat. Eighty men were killed and three hundred taken prisoner, the rest escaping over the Pool to Toxteth.

Civil war

By the beginning of 1644 John Moore, now a Colonel in the Parliamentary army, was appointed Governor of Liverpool and the defences of the town were strengthened. A ditch nine feet deep and thirty-six feet wide, with an earth rampart behind it, enclosed the town from the east end of Dale Street down to the river. Where the streets joined the river there were barricades and at the opposite ends, where they ran into open country, massive gates defended with cannon were built. Earthworks, cannon and guns protected the Pool and the castle and a regiment of foot soldiers and a troop of horse were posted to the town, the burgesses also being conscripted for guard duties.

Discipline was strict and Colonel Moore proved himself a hard and unscrupulous man who, with his family, soon came to be heartily disliked. In fact a young Puritan, who acted as his secretary for a time, wrote that Moore's family "was such an hell upon earth as was utterly intolerable".

Bristol was still in Royalist hands and the Parliamentary ships from the Mersey constantly harried the sea-borne Royalist

supplies. The King had asked the Marquess of Ormonde to send English troops from Ireland. By the end of 1643 3,000 managed to land at Chester, but before they had advanced far into Lancashire they were routed by Parliament armies at the battle of Nantwich. Half were taken prisoner and most of the survivors changed sides and enlisted with the Parliamentary army.

Lathom House was still holding out, the defence being directed by the brave Countess of Derby, but by April, 1644, she was hard pressed, with one Parliamentary army advancing from Bolton and John Moore's force threatening from Liverpool.

The main Royalist army was trapped in York, surrounded by a force of Scottish troops and the armies of Cromwell and Fairfax, while Newcastle was also in dire need of help against a threatened attack from Scotland. Prince Rupert, however, was at Shrewsbury, and with a force of 10,000 men he made a rapid march north.

The very name of Prince Rupert and his cavalry struck terror into the hearts of most English soldiers. When news reached the Roundheads advancing from Bolton that he was on the way they turned back from Lathom House, hoping to reach the security of Bolton again, but Prince Rupert was too quick for them. He reached Bolton first, captured the town and marched on to Wigan and Liverpool.

Moore had also withdrawn from the attack on Lathom House and was busy adding to the defences of Liverpool, ordering great sacks of Irish wool to be heaped on top of the ramparts, as a further protection against gun-fire.

By 7th June Prince Rupert was in sight of Liverpool. In his first fierce assault he lost 1,500 men and was repulsed. He brought up his heavy guns and after a long bombardment made a second assault. Again he was thrown back.

He had no time to lose. Messages were reaching him from York and Newcastle, appealing for help. At last, on 12th June, the Prince decided on a surprise night attack. It was led by the brother of Lord Molyneux, who knew every path and alley in the town. Silently, at dead of night, he led the soldiers through the fields north of the town, towards the Old Hall. By three o'clock, the darkest hour before dawn, they had reached the gun-shattered ramparts protecting it. Cautiously they made their way over them and through the ruins of the outbuildings of the Old Hall. To their astonishment they found them deserted.

Without warning the people of Liverpool, Colonel Moore, knowing that he could not hold out much longer against Prince Rupert's army, had fled with most of the garrison, embarked them on ships anchored in the Mersey and sailed away.

He had left only four hundred Roundhead troops in the castle and as Prince Rupert's men advanced into the town they joined with the people of Liverpool in bitter street fighting which went on for hours. The Royalists killed "almost all they met with, to the number of 360 and among them . . . several that never bore arms in their lives, yea, one poor blind man," wrote an eyewitness.

Prince Rupert's men fought their way along Old Hall Street

and Juggler Street and the remnants of the Parliamentary garrison, after surrendering at the High Cross, were imprisoned in the Tower and St Nicholas church.

Prince Rupert took possession of the castle but stayed for only two or three days. Leaving a small garrison and military governor in Liverpool, he pressed on to Ormskirk and Lathom House and then swept on to York. At first he outwitted the Parliamentary armies which were closing in on him. He reached York, but the next day the opposing armies met at Marston Moor. Cromwell was slightly wounded in this battle, but Prince Rupert's army, outnumbered and outmanoeuvred, was beaten. The Prince fled back through Lancashire to Chester, and by the beginning of September Liverpool suffered yet another siege, as Parliamentarians surrounded the town, dug themselves in and prepared to starve out the Royalist garrison.

A few days later Colonel John Moore brought his shiploads of troops back to the Mersey, which meant that the Royalists had no hope of escaping from the castle by the secret tunnel. The cavalier soldiers mutinied, took their own officers prisoner and surrendered.

Once more a Roundhead military governor was installed in the castle and for the people of Liverpool, with their trade and businesses ruined, their homes shattered and hundreds of their little community wounded or dead, the Civil War was over.

At the battle of Naseby the following year, the King finally surrendered to the Scots and was later handed over to Parliament and brought to trial, Colonel Moore being one of the judges who condemned him to death. From the time of his execution in 1649 until 1660 England was ruled by the Commonwealth, headed by Oliver Cromwell.

During these eleven years Cromwell reconquered Ireland, leaving behind more smouldering hatred of the English, for the Irish endured the most terrible sufferings from many of the Roundheads.

Shipwrights were making heavier ships by this time and the men-of-war which Cromwell used to escort his troopships to

Ireland were too big for the Pool, so he used Milford Haven as his port of embarkation instead of Liverpool.

The people of Liverpool began slowly to recover but they had suffered much and in addition had endured several outbreaks of plague. They put in a large claim for damage to life and property during the fighting and in 1649 were awarded £10,000 compensation, but three years later this was changed to the promise of a grant of land in Ireland which they never received. They did receive help for a certain amount of rebuilding, however, and it was during the Commonwealth that the town was made into a separate parish. This meant that the tithes which they had hitherto paid to Walton church now went to the upkeep of their own church of St Nicholas and the stipend of the vicar.

There was little trade with Ireland at this time and only a small beginning of the West Indies tobacco trade. The town grew weary of military dictatorship. They resented their loss of self-government and disliked the military governor. They were angry when soldiers exercised their right to enter their homes, to ensure that they were observing the Sabbath in the manner decreed by Parliament. They protested bitterly when soldiers were billeted on them. They never forgave John Moore for deserting them when Prince Rupert was attacking the town, and the prestige of the Moore family never recovered. After eleven years, Liverpool, like nearly every other borough throughout the country, was ready to welcome the restoration of Charles II in 1660.

5. RICHES FROM THE WEST INDIES

During the Commonwealth it had become clearly established that although Liverpool was a valuable trading port it was unsuitable for a naval base. In 1652 the Commissioners of Ireland had told the Council of State in London that "the going of your ships of war into those ports (Liverpool and Chester) to victual or upon any other account is of very great prejudice to your service, they being, it seems, very difficult ports to get out of . . ." and again "we desire they have express orders not to go into Chester or Liverpool water, lest they be barred up there for three months at least".

At Chester, the Dee was rapidly becoming unusable. Early in the seventeenth century it was described as "the worse river in the Kingdom" and during the first years of the Restoration the Mayor of Chester was lamenting that the river had become so choked with sand that there was not enough water "to bring up a vessel of two tunns". By 1660, therefore, Liverpool was formally declared independent of any customs claims Chester might still try to bring and a few years later the boundaries of the port were clearly defined.

Yet for the first year or two after the return of Charles II Liverpool had little business. There was a certain amount of coastal trade with Bristol and some even as far as London, but the Irish trade had practically ceased, for Ireland had been reduced to a desert. Thousands of her people had been killed in the fighting or died of starvation or the plague, while others had emigrated. By 1665 there were hardly any sheep or cattle in the country and Dublin had no ships at all. Ireland was ruined.

Liverpool, too, had suffered grievous casualties during the

three sieges of the Civil War, so that although she had received many Irish immigrants, her total population had increased hardly at all and was still only about 2,000.

Now, however, a sequence of national events combined to bring about a rapid change in Liverpool's fortunes.

Holland had for long been our trade rival in the East, the West Indies, West Africa and New England. Within four years of Charles II's accession war broke out. The battle of Lowestoft, in 1665, was a victory for the English, but the Dutch were not defeated. They sought help from France and the war intensified. 1665 was the year of the terrible plague of London, when two-thirds of the population fled from the city, and of those who remained nearly half perished; when the great fire broke out the following year, many terrified citizens thought it had been caused by an invasion of the Dutch and French.

For London merchants whose living lay in the port of London the position was serious and many decided that it would be safer to move their businesses to the ports of the west and south-west. Some arrived in Exeter and Bristol and many in Liverpool. Then the French reorganized their navy and made their Atlantic base at Brest. This meant that even the south-west ports of England were in danger. Bristol became safer than Exeter and Liverpool considerably safer than Bristol, for ships from Liverpool could reach the Atlantic by the northern passage, round the north coast of Ireland.

Despite the devastation which Ireland had suffered, after a few years her trade recovered remarkably quickly and by the end of the 1660s Liverpool was busy again and had built many new ships for the passage to Dublin. Nor did the wars and national disasters affect England's trade farther afield for long; during the 1660s and 1670s it grew steadily, but it was strictly controlled. The great trading companies such as the East India Company, the Levant Company, the Africa Company and the newly-formed Hudson's Bay Company, of which Prince Rupert was the first governor, worked under a licence known as a monopoly. It was like a closed shop in a trade union and anyone who tried to trade independently in these regions was known as an interloper and ran the risk of having his cargo seized and confiscated. Trade with the West Indies and the American colonies was not restricted in this way, however, although the customs officers at the English ports kept a strict watch on all imports.

Our stake in North America and the West Indies was growing steadily, for in 1663 English settlers had founded the colonies of North and South Carolina, which had been named after the King, and the buccaneer from South Wales, Henry Morgan, was making the West Indies safe from a threatened Spanish attack from the South American mainland, for he had been given the status of a privateer. This gave his piratical adventures the blessing of the government, provided he attacked only ships which were enemies of the realm.

Irish merchants turned their thoughts to the West Indian trade and Liverpool seamen began carrying for them, taking out linen, butter and other produce and returning with tobacco and sugar. There was also a great deal of smuggling, for Liverpool ships could easily cross to Ireland and then continue to the West Indies and back to Ireland or the Isle of Man, with produce that the Liverpool customs never saw.

But for Ireland the good times did not last, for the English government decided to forbid their trade with the West Indies, a move which caused more justifiable anger among the Irish. Then, fearing that Irish produce might affect English farmers, they forbade the import to England of Irish cattle, sheep or pigs, beef, mutton, butter and cheese. Ireland was forced to export these provisions to France, Spain and the Netherlands and also to buy from these countries the commodities she had formerly imported from England through Liverpool. Before 1663 Ireland had imported £200,000 worth of goods from England but by 1675 this figure had been reduced to only £20,000.

Liverpool lost her Irish trade but quickly increased her West Indian business, taking out mainly textiles and returning with sugar and tobacco.

In 1668 a "Mr Smith, a sugar baker of London", who had

come to Liverpool to escape the dangers of the capital, built Liverpool's first sugar refinery, renting a piece of land on the north side of Dale Street from the Moore family and putting up a building "forty feet square and four storeys high", and from this time the town became the most important centre for sugar refining in the country.

The import of tobacco also increased steadily, rivalling and eventually outstripping that of Bristol. James I had hated the habit of tobacco smoking. He called it an "ignoble habit, reducing a man to the level of a chimney, and rendering him liable to melancholia". High import duties were imposed, but as the habit of smoking spread despite the royal disapproval, the import duties proved such a valuable source of revenue that the official view changed. Far from being a cause of melancholia, it was now said to be a cure for it, particularly when "accompanied by psalm singing"; and as tobacco is a slight narcotic, it was recommended to make people "less turbulent and inclined to sedition".

By 1671, when the tobacco revenue had reached £100,000 a year, people in England were forbidden to try to grow it for themselves.

At this time Liverpool had sixty-five trading ships, but they were still very small, for their total tonnage was only 2,600.

Peace between England and Holland was negotiated in 1667, the only gain to England being the acquisition of New Amsterdam, the Dutch settlement in North America, close to our New England colonies, which was renamed New York.

Liverpool continued to prosper. In 1673 a visitor to the town wrote that it contained "divers eminent merchants, whose trade and traffic, especially with the West Indies, make it famous" and of Manchester and the other rising industrial centres of Lancashire he said that they "afforded in greater plenty and at reasonabler rates than most places in England such exported commodities proper for the West Indies".

In 1685 Charles II died and his brother, the Catholic James II, succeeded to the throne, but four years later James was forced to abdicate. He fled to Ireland. War broke out between

France and England and French troops and ships joined him in Ireland, to help him try to recover his throne. James's stepsister Mary and her Dutch husband William of Orange had been welcomed to the English throne and William lost no time in assembling an army to fight James.

Liverpool was now in a dangerous position, for French ships were lurking in the Irish Sea. Nevertheless, William decided on the shortest route to Ireland, by way of the Mersey and the Dee to Ulster. Baggage was shipped to Chester by river craft and embarked at Hoylake. Most of the 20,000 Dutch and English troops were embarked at Liverpool, in vessels which joined the convoy at Hoylake. The three hundred troopships, with an escort of eight men-of-war, under the command of Sir Cloudesley Shovell, arrived in Ireland without mishap and the decisive battle of the Boyne, of long and bitter memory, took place on 1st July, 1690. The danger to Liverpool was not over. Later that year fifteen privateers and two French men-of-war "were nigh the north channel for the return of the West India ships belonging to Liverpool", but by the following year the fighting in Ireland was over and James II had fled to France.

Liverpool took no active part in the Irish campaign and this was the last time that the city or the neighbouring anchorage at Hoylake were used for an operation of this kind. War with France continued intermittently until 1815, but henceforth the North Passage was safe, except for the inevitable piracy, and Liverpool's trade continued to develop and expand.

A fundamental reason for her continuing success, apart from her geographical position, was the increasing production of Manchester. Manchester made Liverpool by supplying her with exports and Liverpool made Manchester by providing the transport to Manchester's markets.

With the decline of the Irish trade, Manchester had suffered from a shortage of flax for linen. The manufacturers were already receiving small quantities of cotton from London, which was imported by the Levant Company and bought mainly for making wicks for candles, a vital commodity. At

the same time, the East India Company was importing cotton
fabrics from India, which became very fashionable when
Queen Anne began wearing them. A weaver in Manchester
now had the idea of mixing a linen warp thread with a weft of
"cotton wool". The next step was to weave cloth entirely
from cotton and this cotton cloth from Manchester became
very popular, but the cotton still had to come from London,
and the importers could supply it only after they had met the
demands of the candle-makers. Moreover, the East India
Company began to raise objections, wondering if their imports
of Indian woven cotton were going to suffer.

About this time, colonists in the West Indies found the
cotton plant growing wild. They began to experiment with its
cultivation and occasionally, in the cargoes of rum, sugar and
tobacco which they despatched to Bristol, Liverpool and London, they included a few bags of cotton, in the hope of finding
a market for it. Merchants from Manchester and south Lancashire were soon making the long journey south, by pack-horse
trains, to Bristol or London, in order to pick up any consignments of this West Indies cotton that were available. The damp
climate of Lancashire was particularly suited for the handling of
cotton, and before long Liverpool had become the principal
port for its arrival.

By the end of the seventeenth century the population of
England and Wales was about four and a half million, of whom
half a million were living in London. The other towns and
cities were very small indeed compared with London, the three
biggest being by now Bristol, Norwich and Liverpool, though
none of them had a population of more than five thousand.
Nevertheless, for Liverpool this meant that her population had
more than doubled in forty years and a great many more
houses had to be built.

They were no longer the simple, timbered dwellings of
Tudor and early Jacobean times, for this style of building,
certainly for the prosperous merchants, had given place
to brick and stone houses in the Classical style of the
Italian Renaissance, first introduced in and about London by

Inigo Jones and developed during the Restoration years by Christopher Wren.

Around Liverpool's original seven streets many more now appeared, several created by Sir Edward Moore, son of the hated John Moore, including Moor Street, parallel with Water Street, Fenwick Street, Fenwick's Alley and Bridge's Alley. Lord Molyneux cut a street through the castle orchard which is now known as Lord Street. Alderman Preeson, who lived in a house on the edge of the castle ditch, is commemorated in Preeson's Row. James Street was named after Roger James, Sir Thomas Street after Sir Thomas Johnson.

Streets were also built on the waste land. There had been much controversy over the ownership of this land, which the town declared to be their property. Lord Molyneux once more tried to claim it but failed, and arrangements were made whereby he gave up his last, lingering feudal rights over the town. He still remained hereditary Constable of the Castle but no garrison was kept there and when, a few years later, he was accused of complicity in a Jacobite rebellion, he was deprived of this office and the castle was bought by the Corporation.

A new generation of prosperous, independent merchants had arisen in Liverpool and all traces of feudalism now disappeared. Colonel Moore had died in 1650 and his son and heir, Sir Edward Moore, had inherited the Moore property and became Liverpool's principal ground-landlord. With the Restoration, he found himself with debts of £10,000 and as a Parliamentarian his property was in danger of confiscation. However, he had married the daughter of a staunch Royalist, Sir William Fenwick, and for her sake and that of her children no action was taken. The Fenwicks had lost a great deal of money during the Civil War and much of the remainder went to pay the Moore debts.

Edward was a bitter, intractable man. He quarrelled with the Town Council, who refused to countenance many of his building projects, and died in 1678, when only forty-four years of age, leaving a son who became a feckless spendthrift. He

View of Liverpool, 1680

mortgaged the Moore property and saved himself from bankruptcy only by marrying a rich wife, but by 1718 he had sold all his Lancashire property and departed to the south, thus breaking the long link of his family with Liverpool.

St Nicholas church had become too small for the growing population and the Corporation built a second church, St Peter's, on the waste land beyond the Pool. St Nicholas was still maintained, with its own rector, and a few years later Charles II, anxious to permit freedom of worship to the Nonconformists, allowed a Nonconformist chapel to be built in South Castle Street.

Until the end of the century the Mayor and the Common Council of Liverpool were Royalist and Anglican, but then the more liberal element in the town, some of whom were Non-

LIVERPOOL
TOWER

WATER
STREET

TOWN
HALL

CASTLE

conformist, gained power, and it was these people who, in the next century, were to be known as Whigs.

In 1673 Liverpool's first important building appeared, a new Town Hall to replace John Crosse's little Common Hall, which by now was a hundred and fifty years old. It stood in the middle of the market place, looking up Castle Street, and contained a council chamber and a banqueting hall. It was raised on a colonnade of arches and in the covered area below was an exchange, where wholesale merchants could arrange the purchase and sale of goods and commodities.

Council meetings were held regularly on the first Wednesday of every month and were conducted with great dignity and solemn ceremony, the Mayor, the bailiffs, the aldermen and the common councillors all wearing their special robes of office. Civic banquets, with a fine display of the borough's silver plate, were frequently held during these prosperous days, to celebrate important occasions such as fairs and elections, although by now there were too many freemen in the town for them all to be invited.

Liverpool, with its population of 5,000, was a delightful place in 1700. The men were wearing long, curling wigs at this time, with elegant, knee-length coats, cloth breeches and silk neck-cloths, the women tight bodices and wide, hooped skirts. That valiant traveller, Celia Fiennes, whose accounts of her long journeys on horseback or by coach give such a vivid picture of England at the turn of the century, wrote: "Liverpool, which is in Lancashire is built just on the river Mersey, mostly new built houses of brick and stone after the London fashion; the first original was a few fishermen's houses and now is grown to a large fine town . . . there are a great many Dissenters in the town; its a very rich trading town, the houses of brick and stone built high and even, that a streete quite through looks very handsome, the streetes well pitched; there are abundance of persons you see very well dress'd and of good fashion; the streetes are fair and long, its London in miniature as much as ever I saw any thing."

6. SLAVES FOR THE NEW WORLD, TRADE FOR EUROPE

People who were born and grew up in Liverpool during the first part of the eighteenth century lived through times of continuing and rapid change. The Moore family had departed and much of their property had been bought by the Earl of Derby. The town had bought its independence from the Molyneux family and was free to develop and build as it pleased.

Liverpool had become an independent parish because "many people coming from London at the time of the Sickness, and of the Fire, several Ingenious Men settled in Liverpool; which encouraged them to Trade to the Plantations, and other Places; which occasioned sundry other Tradesmen to come and settle there: which hath so enlarged their Trade, that from scarce paying the Sallary of the Officers of the Customs, it is now the Third part of the Trade of England, and pays upwards of £50,000 per Annum to the King: and by reason of such Encrease of Inhabitants, many new streets are built, and still in building; and many Gentlemens Sons of the Counties of Lancaster, Yorkshire, Staffordshire, Cheshire, and North-Wales, are put Apprentices in the Town. . . ."

Several more sugar refineries were built in and around the town and industries including ship-building, rope-making, glass, metal crafts and pottery were established, using coal from the mines of South Lancashire. In 1670 the rock salt of Cheshire had been discovered and formed yet another valuable export for the Mersey, but more valuable than all these was the incoming trade of tobacco, now being grown in increasing quantities in Virginia, and sugar and cotton from the West Indies, with Manchester goods being sent in exchange.

In 1700 Liverpool owned 70 vessels employing 800 seamen and by 1751 she owned 220 vessels employing 3,319 seamen. The population increased as rapidly as the trade. By 1750 it had reached 25,000 and by 1800 nearly 80,000.

The new, commercial Liverpool was staunchly Whig and loyal to the Hanoverians, so that the two Jacobite rebellions affected the town very little. In 1715 the Old Pretender landed in Scotland, but the Whig Argylls outmatched his 6,000 Highland supporters at the first clash and he fled back to France. There were wholesale arrests among his supporters, many of whom were condemned to transportation to the colonies. A large number were taken there by Liverpool merchants. Sir Thomas Johnston, for example, obtained a contract to transport 637 prisoners at £1 a head. They were carried in nine boats, but in one of them the prisoners revolted, captured the boat and put it into a French port.

The 1745 rebellion of the Old Pretender's son, Charles Edward Stuart, was more serious, for after his landing on Eriskay, with only seven companions, a number of the Highland clans rallied to him. His first battle, at Prestonpans, was a victory, and after a few triumphant weeks at Holyrood Palace, he crossed the border and marched south with an army of 6,000, by way of Carlisle, Lancaster and Manchester.

Liverpool raised a regiment, the Liverpool Blues, to fight for King George II, and seven volunteer companies began looking to the defences of the town.

Bonnie Prince Charlie, hoping to gain supporters on the way, continued his march south through Lancashire and reached as far as Derby, but with every mile the support grew less. Catholic Lancashire sent only one squire. Manchester offered £2,000 but although they sent a regiment of recruits to join him, they did not arrive. From Carlisle to Derby hardly two hundred men joined the Prince and when he heard that three English armies were advancing on him and that Scotland had reaffirmed her allegiance to George II, the campaign which had begun with such high hopes collapsed and he fled back to Scotland and exile, leaving many of his followers to face their trial. Whig Liverpool was the place chosen and the Tower was filled with prisoners, many of whom were sentenced to transportation and forced labour in the colonies. Once again Liverpool merchants gained business and made a handsome profit. In one case £1,000 was charged for the transportation of 130 men, and merchants also received a commission on their sale to the plantation owners. The more dangerous rebels were sentenced to death, at least four of them being publicly hanged on Gallowsfield, between London Road and Islington.

Yet this survival of medievalism did not disrupt the development of eighteenth-century culture in Liverpool, much of which was in sharp contrast to many persisting evils. There was a great deal of building at this time, to house the increasing

The Exchange and Town Hall, 1754

population. The Town Hall of 1673 was now too small for all the business which had to be transacted in it and by 1754 the beautiful Georgian Exchange and Town Hall were built, designed by John Wood, who had planned the centre of fashionable Bath. At first the new Town Hall was a simple, domed block. The ground floor was used as a merchants' exchange and the council chamber, banqueting hall and other offices were on the first floor. Many additions have since been made, but John Wood's central structure still survives, despite the fire of 1795.

The Corporation bought Lord Derby's Tower, part of which was turned into a prison, while the chapel was converted into an assembly room where grand balls were sometimes held. The ladies used to arrive at these balls wearing long cloaks and pattens to protect their shoes from the muddy streets. These pattens were wooden soles held over the instep by a strap, and the soles were mounted on an iron ring which kept the shoes above the mud, for as late as the 1750s even the wealthiest Liverpool merchants did not yet possess their own coaches, although in and around London, where the roads were better, they had been commonplace for nearly a hundred years.

The castle was finally demolished in 1725. On part of the site a fish market was built and on another part St George's church, which has since been pulled down. St Thomas's church in Park Lane was also built about the same time and St Paul's a little later, in 1819.

Building development extended southwards and such streets as Hanover Street, Park Lane and Duke Street were planned, with Georgian mansions in which lived the leading merchant families. Squares of attractive terraced houses, so characteristic of Georgian planning, were also laid out, as, for example, Williamson Square, Clayton Square, Cleveland Square, Wolstenholme Square and St Paul's Square, and there were delightful gardens, known as Ladies' Walks, both at the north of the town, adjoining Old Hall Street, and to the south, along Duke Street.

There had been a small theatre in Drury Lane by the beginning of the century but in 1762 the elegant Theatre Royal was opened in Williamson Square. When Derrick, who was master of ceremonies at the Pump Room at Bath, visited Liverpool in 1760 he said that the merchants seemed "genteel in their address" and their ladies, whom he had seen at the fortnightly assembly at the Town Hall, were "elegantly accomplished and perfectly well-dressed". He approved the food and drink which was offered him and reported that there were three good inns in the town, where "for tenpence a man dines elegantly at an ordinary, consisting of ten or a dozen dishes".

Theatre Royal, 1762

Yet unfortunately this was by no means the whole of the story and there was an uglier side to it. The Town Council, staunchly Whig, was determined to keep its party in power. With the end of feudalism, both in practice and thought, at the end of the previous century, men had been able to acquire the privileges of freemen, which had included the right to vote and become members of the Assembly, by payment of the necessary fees. Now the arrangement ended. Freemen had once more to be elected, and only those who were known to be Whig were chosen. This meant that the Council acquired an increasingly despotic power and they legislated only for the benefit of themselves and their growing businesses. They took no responsibility for the welfare of the ordinary people and the amenities of the growing town, such as its lighting and cleaning and the provision of schools and hospitals and homes for the aged, the sick and the poor. They considered these matters no concern of theirs and when, with the awakening of a social conscience throughout the country, they had to be considered, separate bodies were created in the town to deal with them.

This was a violent, cruel and corrupt age, for all the elegance and artistic achievements of architecture, music, literature and painting. As wealth increased, so did the poverty of the labouring classes. The oppression of the poor, who, with increasing urbanization, lost their stake in the countryside and became increasingly dependent on the whims of employers, was as dire as at any time in England's history, and the old friendship which, during the sixteenth and seventeenth centuries, had existed between master and servant, disappeared.

This was the age of the press gang and transportation, the stocks, the whipping-post and the ducking-stool, and public hanging for such minor crimes as the stealing of a few shillings or a sheep. Progress and reform were checked because people were taught to believe that their good fortune or ill-luck were all part of a divine plan which it was wrong to question.

The famous Liverpool families of the early eighteenth century included the Norrises, Clevelands and Claytons, all of whom sent Whig members to Parliament, and the most famous of them all was the tobacco merchant, Sir Thomas Johnston, who was member for Liverpool from 1701 to 1727. Then his parliamentary career ended abruptly for, along with other Liverpool merchants, he was involved in a scandal over the evasion of customs' duties on tobacco imports and accused of bribery, which, in fairness to Sir Thomas, one must concede was a common enough practice. He resigned his seat, owing £18,000, and was offered the post of collector of customs in

Virginia, but the appointment seems to have been a sinecure, for there is no record of his ever going to Virginia. He retired to London on a small pension, but did not live long after his downfall, for he died there in 1728, with his debts still unpaid.

During the earlier years of his career, however, Sir Thomas served Liverpool well, for it was through his energy and foresight that the first wet dock was built.

Sailing ships were becoming larger. For the Irish trade they were still under forty tons but for the Atlantic crossing they were now anything from ninety to two hundred and fifty tons, with a few as much as three hundred, and it was becoming increasingly difficult to accommodate them in the shallow, tidal Pool. The river itself was dangerous because of its tidal range, its strong currents and rock bottom. Ships had to unload part of their cargo in the Hoylake anchorage of Wirral until they were light enough "to sail over the Flats to Liverpool".

To solve the problem, Sir Thomas Johnston consulted Thomas Steers, the engineer who had helped make the first English wet dock at Rotherhithe, London, in 1700. Steers began work on the Liverpool dock in 1710, using the broad mouth of the Pool. The upper reaches, thereby cut off from the river, were closed and partially filled in. Here, in later years, Paradise Street and Whitechapel were built. The new dock had accommodation for eighty to a hundred ships and was an immediate success. Steers was appointed Dockmaster and in 1718 he added a dry dock to the north. In 1721 a new Customs House was built. A wooden pier was added in 1725 and by 1734 work had begun on the Salthouse dock, intended primarily for the Cheshire salt trade, for a great salt works had for some time existed on the waste ground south of the Pool.

With the buoying of the channel, Liverpool became one of the safest and most up-to-date ports in England, but it was still isolated from the rest of the country inland, for the roads were appalling. Inland transport of goods was still, when possible, made by river, for pack-horse trains were slow and the roads often too rough for carts.

River beds were constantly being scoured and deepened to

help water transport and in 1694 Thomas Patten, a merchant of Warrington, began improving the Mersey between Warrington and Runcorn. By 1701 he had built his own quay at Warrington, to receive his consignments of tobacco, which then went by cart to Stockport, by pack-horse to Doncaster and then by river to Hull.

The next step was to try to establish a water connection between Liverpool and Manchester, "for the river to Manchester is very capable of being made navigable at a very small charge," wrote Patten.

By 1720 this had been achieved, the rivers Mersey and Irwell having been scoured and deepened and made navigable from Liverpool to Manchester. Traffic was soon passing regularly along the winding fifty-mile stretch of the improved waterway and the proprietors, known as "Mersey and Irwell Navigation", had the monopoly of water commerce between the two towns for many years to come. Things did not always run smoothly, however. In dry weather there were delays through a shortage of water and in rainy seasons too much water damaged the installations. Locks and weirs had to be constantly maintained and cuts made to shorten distances on some of the more winding stretches.

At the same time, roads were improved. The government did not take responsibility for their building and upkeep. Each section of road was the responsibility of the parish through which it passed and it was the duty of the surveyor of roads, appointed by the magistrates for each parish, to see that the local residents provided the labour or the money for their upkeep. As most people resented having to pay for the maintenance of roads, through which travellers living outside the parish could pass, they avoided their obligations whenever possible and, despite the work of General Wade on the Highland roads after the 1715 rebellion, elsewhere in the country they remained appalling.

Then the Turnpike Trusts were formed by groups of people who undertook the control and repair of certain stretches of road and charged a toll to the users. Each Trust had to be legalized by a special Act of Parliament and throughout the eighteenth century hundreds of these Acts were passed. It was not unknown for the unfortunate toll-keeper to be beaten up and cheated of his dues by unscrupulous travellers, but the system did bring about a gradual improvement in roads, although as late as 1770 Arthur Young, writing of the road from Preston to Wigan, said: "I know not in the whole range of the language, terms sufficiently expressive to describe this infernal road . . . let me most seriously caution all travellers who may accidentally purpose to travel this terrible country to avoid it as they would the devil; for a thousand to one but they break their neck or their limbs by overthrows or breaking down. They will meet here with ruts, which I actually measured four feet deep. . . . I passed three carts broken down in these eighteen miles of execrable memory."

Not before time, the road from Manchester to Liverpool was reconstructed and the journey made considerably easier for freight wagons and pack-horses. The first passenger coaches claimed to cover the thirty-five miles in twelve hours; Mersey and Irwell Navigation declared that the journey by water took much the same time, but disillusioned merchants said it took much nearer eighteen hours and not infrequently thirty-six.

In 1759 the Duke of Bridgewater instructed his engineer, James Brindley, to cut a canal between Manchester and the Duke's collieries at Worsley, seven miles away; and in 1761, when the first barge of coal was shipped along the new canal from the mines to the city, the cost of transport was so reduced that the price of coal in Manchester fell from sevenpence to threepence halfpenny a hundredweight.

The Duke's next plan was to build a canal from Manchester to Liverpool. Despite strong opposition from the proprietors of Mersey and Irwell Navigation, the plan was approved by Parliament, and by 1776 the locks had been completed at Runcorn and the canal opened to the public from Manchester to the Mersey estuary.

The transport of goods by road had been charged at the rate of forty shillings a ton. By Mersey and Irwell Navigation it was twelve shillings a ton. But on the Duke's canal the cost was, from the outset, only six shillings a ton. So the competitors began a hasty revision of their charges and a price war began.

Nevertheless, the Duke's canal was so successful that, before long, canals were being built across the rapidly developing regions of southern Lancashire and the West Midlands, including the Leeds–Liverpool canal and the Grand Junction canal, joining the Mersey to the Trent, and they were soon being built throughout the entire country.

Liverpool prospered and her merchants grew wealthy, particularly those who, by now, had become deeply involved in the slave trade.

Europeans had been engaged in the slave trade for several centuries before Liverpool entered the business. By the middle of the fifteenth century the Portuguese, exploring the West African coast, had reached Sierra Leone, and Portuguese merchants had established trading colonies on the Cape Verde Islands. They sent Negro slaves to Spain and Portugal, to work on agricultural land which had only recently been abandoned by Arabs and Moors during their centuries of occupation.

Unfortunately for the Negroes, the year that the last of the Moors were expelled from Granada was also the year that Christopher Columbus landed in the West Indies and took possession of them for their Catholic Majesties of Spain. There was very little native labour in the islands and the Portuguese were soon extending their trade in slaves by shipping them across the Atlantic for the Spaniards, to work on the new Spanish plantations.

These slaves were drawn mostly from Senegal and Gambia or from Benin and the region of the Niger Delta. Later, when the Portuguese were developing their colonies in Brazil, they shipped Negroes from the Congo and Angola.

The first Englishman to visit West Africa was the father of Sir John Hawkins. He had no interest in slaves. In fact, slavery was abhorrent to all Englishmen early in the sixteenth century and the Navy scorned the French and Spanish practice of using galley slaves to man their ships.

Within the next few years more Englishmen risked the hazardous journey to West Africa, to trade in ivory and gold dust. Some never returned, but others survived the dangers of the malarial coast and the terrible storms in the Gulf of Benin, where, as the old sailors' song had it: "For one that comes out there are forty stay in."

In 1562 Sir John Hawkins visited West Africa and, until war broke out with Spain in 1588, he carried Negroes from West Africa to the New World for Spain, the first Englishman to engage himself in the slave trade.

The slaves in these relatively early days of the European trade were for the most part already prisoners, held by tribal chiefs after inter-tribal wars. The chiefs or their agents supplied them to European slavers, arguing that as the wretched men and women would probably have been put to death anyway, the transaction was of benefit to everyone.

It was not until the reign of Charles II that the City of London financed the Royal Africa Company for trade with West Africa. The Royal Africa Company took woollen and other manufactured goods to West Africa, sending back to London ivory, redwood and gold dust. It also dealt in slaves, which it claimed to supply "at a moderate rate", for by this time Spain, Portugal, Holland, France and England were all in urgent need of labour for their colonies in the New World, some of which were virtually uninhabited. In fact, one of the main reasons for the continued interest in Africa now was for its Negro labour supply, for alternative supplies of pepper had been found in the East Indies and the gold in Spanish America was far more abundant than in West Africa.

By 1600 about 500,000 Negroes had been landed in the Americas and the West Indies. The sugar plantations were particularly successful, but sugar cane cultivation needed a great deal of labour. As the population of Europe increased, so did the demand for sugar, with the result that an increasing number of slaves were needed. During the next century, nearly three million were transported.

However, the affairs of the Royal Africa Company did not

prosper. The whole coast was infested with pirating traders who "by their sinister traffic . . . lowered the price of European goods in Africa and rose the price of African goods".

The situation was impossible to control and in the end the English government decided to make the Guinea trade free to all English merchants, whether they were members of the company or not, provided they paid a ten per cent levy to the company for the upkeep of its ports and fortifications. The monopoly was at last broken and Bristol merchants, many of whom had been illicitly trading tobacco for slaves for many years past, now entered the business on a large scale, in competition with London traders.

The slave trade became more sinister and dreadful than ever. Up till this time the slaves, as we have seen, had been mainly prisoners who otherwise would have been put to death. Native dealers obtained them from the local chiefs and brought them down to the coast. By seventeenth-century standards, their conditions of transport had been reasonably good and certainly not much worse than those of the sailors themselves. There had been no kidnapping, for once the dealers had lost faith in a trader they would obviously not do business with him again; and they could easily retaliate by destroying the company's small shore settlements and stores.

Now, however, competition was fiercer and altogether more violent. Slaves were in such demand that they represented sources of great wealth to both sellers and buyers. Any lingering feelings of humanity disappeared and there was increasing corruption and cruelty. Native dealers at times promoted inter-tribal wars in order to create prisoners for sale. Traders making a single journey to the coast, and having no connection with any shore establishment, had nothing to lose by attempting a kidnapping foray, for they could quickly slip out to sea again and the Africans had no means of exacting retribution.

With the opening years of the eighteenth century came an appalling intensification of the slave trade, in which England was soon playing a leading part. By the Treaty of Utrecht of 1713, she won the sole right to transport Negro slaves to the

Spanish colonies at the rate of a minimum of 4,800 slaves a year, and as many more as could be procured.

In addition to the enormous supplies of slaves absorbed by Spain, England was now importing thousands of slaves to her own colonies in the West Indies. Between 1680 and 1780 we sent more than two million slaves across the Atlantic to English plantations. The total number of Negro men and women taken each year from Guinea alone, throughout the eighteenth century, has been estimated at over 100,000 and between fifteen and twenty per cent of them died during the terrible voyage across the Atlantic.

The biggest problem in developing England's overseas trade was finding sufficient capital to finance the ships and their cargoes for the first journeys. Early in the eighteenth century a great many trading companies were formed in London, but after the failure of the South Sea Company in 1720, many London merchants became wary of investing their money in these ventures.

Bristol had been second to London in the slave trade; by 1709 it had fifty-seven slavers in service and was growing wealthy on the proceeds. Bristol merchants now took advantage of the London recession and very soon were in the lead with the slave-carrying trade. They took iron, brass and woollen goods to Africa and bartered them for slaves. They carried the slaves across the Atlantic for sale and returned to Bristol with cargoes of tobacco, sugar and rum.

Liverpool saw the opportunities that Bristol was seizing and determined not to be left out of the scramble for wealth. Yet her merchants, though prospering, still had not the large sums of money necessary to equip their ships, buy the cargoes of Manchester goods especially designed for the African market and wait twelve months for the return of their money, for this was the average time for the round trip from Liverpool to West Africa, across the Atlantic to America and back again to Liverpool. They had to set to work to devise a means of raising the necessary money.

7. THE SLAVE TRADE

The solution to the problem, though illegal, was simple. The merchants of Liverpool worked their way into the business by first taking Manchester cotton goods direct to the West Indies, where they sold them as contraband to Spanish traders from Cuba and the mainland, who sailed to Jamaica in small schooners and smuggled the goods into the Spanish colonies, free of the three hundred per cent duty imposed by Spain.

Spain protested but it was no easy matter to stop either her own smugglers or the Liverpool pirates. At the height of the smuggling the Liverpool men's annual profit was over a quarter of a million pounds and they soon accumulated the capital for their first slave ships. It was not until 1747 that an Act of Parliament forbade foreign vessels to visit British West Indian ports. This made it more difficult for Spanish smugglers to call at Jamaica but it no longer mattered to the Liverpool merchants, for they now had the money they needed.

As early as 1730, determined to undersell the merchants of Bristol, Liverpool men sent fifteen slave ships to Africa. The captains and crews were not so well paid as the Bristol men. Bristol captains were paid five shillings a day and treated like gentlemen. Liverpool captains received £1 a month and much rougher fare and accommodation. They were hardened, experienced seamen, engaged in a tough and competitive business.

By 1737 Liverpool's fleet of slave ships had risen to thirty-three and by 1752 it was fifty-eight. Bristol and London were still engaged in the trade, but by 1771 only twenty-three slavers sailed from Bristol and fifty-eight from London, while a hundred and seven went from Liverpool.

Although the French, Dutch and Portuguese were all engaged in the slave trade, more than half the slaves carried across the Atlantic were now taken in British ships, most of them sailing from Liverpool.

The Liverpool shipyards were busy building stout, full-rigged ships, which varied in size from 150 to 400 tons. They were loaded with Manchester cottons, mostly dyed in the blues and bright greens which the Africans preferred. Striped loin cloths also found a ready market. The ships were armed with fourteen to twenty guns and then set sail for the shallow creeks and malarial swamps of the west coast, their most important ports of call being Bonny and Old Calabar.

Here are the instructions given to Captain Ambrose Lace, master of the ship *Marquess of Granby*, "ready to sail for Africa and America and back to Liverpool, the 14th April, 1762". ". . . Purchase 550 slaves and lay out £400 in Ivory. Pray mind to be very choice in your slaves. Buy no distempered or old ones . . . after reaching the Leeward Islands [sell the slaves] Guadaloupe or Martinico, or any other of the Leeward Islands whichever is the best market . . . and to have the ship loaden in the following manner: Viz.: about one hundred casks good Mus Sugar for the Ground Tier, the remainder with the First and Second White Sugars, in betwixt Decks with good Cotton and Coffee. . . . Proceed to Jamaica . . . then have the ship loaden in the following manner: Viz.: as much Broad Sound Mahogany as will serve for Dunnage, the Hold filled with the very best Mus Sugar and Ginger and Betwixt Decks with Good Cotton and Pimento and about Ten Puncheons Rum. . . ."

As early as 1693 the Quakers of Pennsylvania had issued an "Exhortation and Caution to Friends Concerning the Buying and Selling of Negroes", and with the passing years others joined in protesting at the wickedness of the trade, but there had been such a radical change in the attitude to slavery amongst most Englishmen since the days of Queen Elizabeth I that the English government, supported by many Churchmen, declared that it was justified because it was the means of bringing the Africans in touch with Christianity. It also brought undreamed-of riches and was accepted as a blessing bestowed on a chosen few by a benign Providence.

John Newton, who in later life was to do so much for the abolition of slavery, was himself the master of a Liverpool slaver about this time. He later wrote: "During the time I was engaged in the slave trade, I never had the least scruple as to its lawfulness. I was upon the whole, satisfied with it, as the appointment Providence had marked out for me. It is, indeed, accounted a genteel employment. . . ."

The high demand for slaves caused increasing corruption amongst the African chiefs and dealers who obtained them. When demand exceeded supply, natives were arrested on false charges, such as theft or witchcraft. Eventually whole villages were attacked. When a slave ship was sighted off the coast, the chiefs would send out their agents with parties of warriors, sometimes 3,000 strong. These raids extended ever farther inland, some reaching as much as two hundred miles from the coast. In the dead of night, sleeping villages were attacked. The huts were set alight and the fleeing, terrified natives captured, stripped naked and strung together. Then they were herded down to the coast. Children were separated from their parents, wives from their husbands. Those who did not survive the long march were left to die. If numbers were still not sufficient, English sailors sometimes undertook raids themselves or kidnapped canoe loads of Africans who were fishing or trading along the coast.

Conditions inside the slave ships were appalling. The slave deck, with scarcely head room for a tall man, was fitted with wooden benches clamped to the floor. The slaves were chained to these benches, which were so close together that each man had little more than a square yard of living space. Sometimes the men were chained in couples, the right leg and arm of one man fastened to the left leg and arm of his partner, so that they could not move or even change their position without hurting each other. A typical slave cabin was forty-six feet long and twenty-five feet wide, into which three hundred and fifty male slaves were packed, and accommodation for the women and children was even more cramped.

Here they waited for weeks and sometimes months, until the slaver had acquired its full complement of victims and was ready to set sail on the long and stormy "Middle Passage" across the Atlantic to the West Indies.

There was little ventilation in the slave cabins and the heat was intolerable. There were a few small portholes and a grating in the roof, which in stormy weather was covered by a tarpaulin.

In fine weather the slaves were allowed on deck, where they received their food, but so many attempted to revolt or commit suicide by throwing themselves overboard that it became the custom to fasten a chain from their shackles to a ring bolt on deck. In bad weather they were allowed up on deck in batches of ten, for a few minutes at a time, just long enough to eat their food before they were sent below again and the next batch was brought up.

They were fed twice a day, at eight o'clock in the morning and four o'clock in the afternoon. Their food was brought in small wooden buckets, ten slaves feeding from each bucket. Half a pint of water was provided at each meal, which the slave had to drink down straight away from the pannikin in which it was offered to him.

Captain William Snelgrave, who in 1734 published an account of his slaving adventures, described the fate of Captain Messerby on an occasion when the slaves had been driven beyond all human endurance. Captain Messerby, "being on the Forecastle of the ship, among the Men-negroes when they were eating their Victuals, they laid hold on him, and beat out his Brains with the little Tubs out of which they eat their boiled rice".

When slaves tried to commit suicide by deliberately starving themselves, they were forcibly fed, and the barbarous *speculum oris*, an instrument specially designed to prise open their jaws, was advertised in Liverpool and sold to the slave ships.

Dr Isaac Wilson, a surgeon on board one of the slavers, described what happened to a slave who finally succeeded in starving himself to death: "Mild means were used to divert him from his resolution; they endeavoured to make him understand that he should have anything he wished for; but he still refused to eat; they then used the cat with as little success; he always kept his teeth so fast, that it was impossible to get anything down; they endeavoured to introduce a *speculum oris*; but the points were too obtuse to enter; and next tried a bolus knife without effect. In this state he was four or five days, when he was brought up as dead, to be thrown overboard."

Dr Wilson found that he was not dead and he was taken below again, in a state of coma. He regained consciousness and asked for water, which he drank, but he still refused to allow himself to be fed, and a few days later he died.

This was the end of the slave trade for Dr Wilson, and yet he maintained that the captain was a man of humanity, who "never allowed anyone to chastise the slaves except himself and the surgeon".

One of the most scandalous affairs was the trip of the slave ship *Zong*, which sailed from West Africa to Jamaica in 1781, with a cargo of 440 slaves. Through bad seamanship on the part of the master, Captain Collingwood, they missed Jamaica and were two months at sea. Food and water ran short and fever and dysentery broke out. Sixty slaves died and many more were dying. Collingwood called his crew together and suggested that the slaves who could obviously not recover should be thrown overboard, for, he said: "If the slaves die on board, the owners will lose, but if we maintain that the slaves were thrown overboard for the preservation of the ship, the underwriters will have to bear the loss."

One hundred and thirty-two slaves were chosen. On the first day, fifty-four were dragged on board and flung into the sea. On the second day forty-two were drowned and on the next day the remaining thirty-six. Ill as they were, they struggled desperately, until the captain ordered them to be shackled with ankle and wrist chains in order to speed their drowning.

Some captains had fairly good records, however. Captain Frazer, for example, was in the trade for twenty years and lost comparatively few slaves, except for a disastrous trip in 1777, when one-fifth of his slaves died of measles, and his last voyage from Bonny to Jamaica, when bad weather and resulting delays caused a shortage of both food and water, and more than a hundred slaves died.

Once the slave ships reached the West Indies, the slaves were washed and made to look as presentable as possible. There were three methods of sale. Sometimes planters had already made a private treaty with the traders. On landing, therefore, a selection of slaves was taken to the planter's office. He chose those who took his fancy and the rest were returned to the ship. A second method of sale was "by scramble". As the slaver entered port, the men slaves were lined up on the main deck, the women on the quarter deck. The buyers waited on the quayside. Then a signal gun was fired from the slaver. The gang plank was lowered and the buyers swarmed on board, quickly choosing the slaves whom they considered most healthy and seizing them until the captain was ready to conclude their purchase.

The slaves who were left behind in this terrifying scramble were taken ashore and sold by the third method, which was public auction in the market place. And those who were too

A slave awaiting sale

ill to be worth a bid were either given away or abandoned.

The profits to be made from the traffic in slaves were very large indeed. Between 1783 and 1793, 878 round trips were made by Liverpool slavers, during which they carried 303,737 slaves from Africa to the West Indies. They sold them for over £15,000,000 and it has been calculated that the profit on the sale of the slaves alone brought Liverpool merchants some

£300,000 a year. In addition, they were able to make profits on the return cargoes of sugar, tobacco, rum and cotton.

Planters who had made a fortune in the West Indian plantations sometimes, on retiring, brought slaves back to England as personal servants and, for a while, it was highly fashionable to have a Negro boy or girl about the household. When they ran away, as they sometimes did, advertisements and rewards for their recovery were published in the newspapers.

In Williamson's *Advertiser* of 17th February, 1758, there appeared, for example, this notice: "Run away from Dent, in Yorkshire, on Monday, the 28th August last, Thomas Anson, a negro man, about 5′ 6″ high, aged 20 years and upwards, and broad set. Whoever will bring the said man back to Dent, or give any information that he may be had again, shall receive a handsome reward from Mr Edmund Sill, of Dent; or Mr David Kenyon, Merchant, in Liverpool."

The traffic in Negro slaves also took place in London, and during the middle years of the eighteenth century some 20,000 were bought and sold at the Royal Exchange, each one branded and wearing a padlock collar, engraved with the name or coat of arms of his owner.

In Liverpool, slaves were sometimes sold on the Goree Piazzas, but never in any great numbers; records show that the most ever offered at one time was eleven.

Towards the end of the eighteenth century increasing attention was being paid to the protests of the abolitionists. America had freed herself from colonial oppression. By 1789 the people of France were ridding themselves of the oppressive landed aristocracy. Freedom was being preached by writers and political philosophers—and it included freedom for the Negro slaves.

John Newton, though he had led a tempestuous youth and had at one time been the despair of his friends and family, was one of the first slave masters to suffer a change of heart. "The office of a gaoler, and the restraints under which I was obliged to keep my prisoners, were not suitable to my feelings; but I considered it as the line of life which God in His providence had allotted me and as a cross which I ought to bear with patience and thankfulness till He should be pleased to deliver me from it," he wrote in later years.

After three voyages, he suffered a severe illness and was advised to retire from the sea. For several years he was tide-surveyor in the port of Liverpool but during this time he was thinking ever more seriously of entering the Church. In 1764, at the age of thirty-eight, he was ordained curate of the little town of Olney in North Buckinghamshire. It was here that he formed his deep friendship with William Cowper and in collaboration with him wrote the Olney Hymns.

He never forgot the plight of the slaves and many other people were by now equally concerned. In 1772, as a result of the agitation of Granville Sharp, a test case was brought concerning a slave who had been ill-treated in England by his English owner, and it was decided by the Lord Chief Justice that no one could be a slave on the territory of the United Kingdom and that once he set foot on British soil he was free and could not be taken back into slavery. This, of course, immediately put a stop to the sale of slaves in London, Bristol and Liverpool, though not yet to their purchase in Africa and transportation across the Atlantic.

In 1780, after sixteen years at Olney, John Newton was invited to become vicar of St Mary Woolnoth in Lombard Street, in the City of London, and it was here that his work for the abolition of slavery achieved practical results. He published his first pamphlet, describing the true conditions of the slave trade, which aroused the interest of William Wilberforce. On his election to Parliament in 1784, Wilberforce began his work for the freedom of the slaves, reaffirming David Hartley's motion which had been defeated in the House of Commons eight years earlier that "the slave trade was contrary to the laws of God and the rights of man". Now Parliament ordered a special investigation, and John Newton was summoned as the most important witness, to give first-hand evidence.

The northern states of America had already agreed not to buy slaves or have any dealings with those concerned in the slave trade, despite the fact that slavery still existed in the cotton plantations of the south.

In 1787 an Anti-Slavery Committee was formed under the presidency of Granville Sharp, and two years later, as the revolution was breaking out in France and the oppressed peoples of Europe were emerging to demand their own freedom, the Committee bought land in Sierra Leone for the resettlement of freed American Negroes. The little colony, only four hundred strong at first, was established at Freetown under the governorship of Zachary Macaulay, father of the historian.

In Liverpool, though a few merchants were sympathetic to the movement, many raged at the folly of destroying a business on which such large fortunes had been based.

In 1788 the states of New York, Massachusetts and Pennsylvania forbade the import of slaves within their boundaries. Two years later Congress forbade citizens of the United States to engage in the trade of supplying foreigners with either slaves or slave-ships, and ordered the states which still employed slaves to ensure that their passages were made under humane conditions.

The founding of the London Missionary Society in 1795, the Colonial Missionary Society in 1799 and the British and Foreign Bible Society in 1804 all helped to strengthen the anti-slavery movement. The French Revolutionary Committee made the slave trade illegal in 1794, the Danes in 1804 and the British in 1807, closely followed by the United States in 1808 and the Dutch in 1814.

So despite the protests and gloomy forebodings of financial ruin, the Liverpool slave trade came to an end.

8. PRIVATEERS, PRESS GANGS AND POTTERS

The long wars with France and Spain, which continued intermittently during the whole of the eighteenth century and the early years of the nineteenth century, had caused many serious setbacks; though the merchants and slave traders had prospered, there were long periods of terrible distress and unemployment in the port amongst the seamen and their families.

Throughout these years, fighting took place both on land and the high seas with mounting intensity, and Liverpool, rapidly becoming Britain's most important port after London, inevitably suffered.

Liverpool merchantmen had to be armed and they were issued with Letters of Marque, which gave them authority to give fight to any enemy ships they encountered. Liverpool also sent out many privateers. These were small private battleships, carefully disguised to look like merchantmen, though they did not carry cargo. Their captains were also given Letters of Marque and were entitled to a large proportion of the spoils, while a third was distributed amongst the crew.

During the War of the Austrian Succession, Liverpool lost 103 vessels, mainly on the way to the West Indies, though some were taken on the African run and others on visits to European ports. Merseyside shipyards were kept busy building new ships, but an increasing number were now being built for Liverpool merchants in America, where there was an abundance of timber.

The most famous of all the privateers during this war was Fortunatus Wright, the son of a Liverpool merchant captain. Fortunatus commanded a privateer cruising in the Mediterranean and between 1744 and 1777 he is said to have captured prizes worth £400,000. When the war ended, in 1748, he retired to Leghorn, but with the outbreak of the Seven Years War in 1756 he was off to sea again, equipping a privateer, the *St George* of Liverpool, with twelve guns and eighty men. After another success against a French ship, which stationed itself outside Leghorn harbour to intercept British merchant shipping, he set sail for England, but on the way his ship foundered and he and his crew were drowned.

This war caused insurance rates for cargo ships to rise so high that trading came almost to a standstill for a while. It cost twelve guineas to insure each £100 worth of goods to Jamaica and twenty-five guineas for the same amount to the Mediterranean. A few merchantmen attempted the journeys in convoy but losses were heavy, the total for Liverpool during the seven years being 97 ships. In 1754 she had 250 ships, but by the following year only 230. By 1758 the number had risen again to 250, but this was a bad year and by 1759 she had only 202. At the end of the war, however, by which time privateers and men-of-war had made the seas safer, the total had risen to 310.

George Campbell of Liverpool equipped several privateers and made a small fortune for himself, while William Hutchinson, who had been Fortunatus Wright's lieutenant in his earlier days, was one of the most successful privateer captains of the war. In June 1757, in the *Liverpool*, equipped with twenty-two guns and two hundred men, he captured a large French ship and brought her back to Liverpool. He recaptured an English ship, chased a French privateer on to the rocks and captured the crew of a fishing schooner. With the help of another English privateer, he captured three more French ships and then, on his own again, seized another three enemy ships. One of them sank, but the other two he brought back to Liverpool with their crews.

Before the end of the war, he had accomplished further daring exploits in the Mediterranean; luckier than Wright, he survived and returned to Liverpool, where he was appointed Water Bailiff and Dockmaster. William Hutchinson lived on until 1801 and was much loved for his kindness and his many philanthropies, particularly to seamen and their families.

Romantic as these adventures may now seem, they involved terrible suffering among the sailors of Liverpool, who in addition to the wartime hazards of their calling, lived in constant dread of the hated press gangs. The press men were often waiting as they disembarked from their merchant ships, to order them into the service of the Royal Navy. Protest was useless. The men were arrested, flogged and herded aboard the

The press gang at work

warships. In 1759, H.M.S. *Vengeance* tried to impress the entire crew of a whaler as it returned home to the Mersey. There was a fight in the Customs House, during which the captain and first mate were captured, though the rest of the crew managed to escape through the windows. A slave-ship then arrived from Jamaica, and the captain of the *Vengeance* impressed almost the entire crew.

It was a hard and brutal age. Conditions below decks in the Royal Navy were appalling and there was always the prospect of a dreaded French prison at the end of the journey. Thousands of Liverpool men suffered this fate during the French wars, and the hardships they endured were often terrible to the point of inhumanity.

Early in the war, the French privateer *Thurot* startled and alarmed Liverpool by appearing uncomfortably close, in the North Channel. Once again, defences were prepared. A battery of guns was set up in the churchyard of St Nicholas and for the next two years the town was on the alert. With the peace of 1763, Liverpool made a quick recovery, only to be faced with more trouble twelve years later, with the outbreak of the American War of Independence. "All commerce with America is at an end," declared one Liverpool writer in 1775. "Our once extensive trade with Africa is at a stand . . . and the docks are full of gallant ships laid up and useless."

The Liverpool Blues, with officers from the regular army, departed for garrison duty in Jamaica; here and elsewhere in the West Indies, American privateers were inflicting terrible damage on Liverpool ships. When John Paul Jones, the most daring of the American privateers, reached as far as England and destroyed shipping at Whitehaven, Liverpool looked again to her shore defences. There was no point, at this juncture, in equipping British privateers, for American overseas trade was very small, and for many months there was great distress and unemployment in Liverpool, with 3,000 sailors hanging about the port, idle, restless and hungry.

When merchants in the Africa trade seized the opportunity of a surplus of labour to reduce the wages of their seamen from thirty shillings a month to twenty shillings, disastrous riots broke out. Nine men were arrested and thrown into the Tower, but a crowd of 2,000 angry, armed sailors besieged it until they were released. Then they stormed through the town, looting shops and taverns and threatening to bombard the Town Hall with cannon. The reign of terror lasted for a week and soldiers had to be sent from Manchester to put an end to it.

In 1778 France joined America against England; though Liverpool shipping was in greater danger than ever there were now plenty of targets for privateers. Within six months Liverpool had equipped 120 privateers to deal with French shipping and in the first five weeks they had captured £100,000 worth of booty. Their richest prize was the French Indiaman *Carnatic*, aboard which was found a box of diamonds valued at £135,000. Throughout the war 3,000 Liverpool men were employed in privateering and French prisoners filled the Tower and the old powder magazine on Brownlow Hill.

After the end of the war in 1783, there were ten years of peace and recovery before the French Revolutionary Wars began. Liverpool, which at first had been sympathetic to the grievances of the revolutionaries, soon joined with most other people in England in disapproval and mounting fear of their violence.

Whiggery, Liberalism and all reforming movements were now regarded with suspicion. People were afraid that they paved the way to revolution, and there was a sharp swing to Toryism. The Liverpool Town Council, which had for so long been Whig, now turned Tory and reaffirmed its loyalty to George III and the Constitution.

Steps were taken to protect Liverpool trade and the privateers were in business yet again. They were so successful that it was not long before French overseas trade practically disappeared and Liverpool merchants were able to resume an almost normal commerce.

By 1799 there were 4,000 French prisoners in Liverpool, many being housed in the new Borough Gaol, but though the Liverpool privateers had achieved so much, ordinary seamen were in greater danger than ever from the press gangs, who were at their most active during the Napoleonic Wars. Merchantmen were frequently boarded by ships of the Royal Navy, brought back to port and their crews impressed for service.

So great was the dread of the press gangs that, on entering the Mersey, sailors would sometimes jump overboard and swim to the Cheshire shore and the safety of Old Mother Redcap's

Old Mother Redcap helps sailors to escape

tavern, for Mother Redcap was a good friend to hunted sailors and had her own secret escape routes for them. Some even declared that an underground passage from her inn led as far away as New Brighton.

After the Battle of Trafalgar, in 1805, the immediate danger of a French invasion of England was over and the English navy was left in command of the seas; though the slave trade was abolished only two years later, Liverpool became busier than she had ever been, for she was now the principal carrier of Manchester textiles and West Indian sugar and tobacco to the whole of Europe. Nor did the abolition of slavery affect production on the plantations, for the Negroes continued to work them, as free men.

Napoleon made one last effort to curtail England's trade, by refusing to allow English vessels to enter any Continental ports. England retaliated by forbidding neutral ships to trade with any countries under Napoleonic sway, unless they had first called at a British port. The result was wholesale smuggling; America objected to the embargo so strongly that, in 1812, she declared war on England, embarking on a fresh series of extremely successful privateering cruises. One American privateer reached the Irish sea and during a cruise of thirty-seven days captured twenty-seven Liverpool ships. Liverpool's business shrank and at one time was down to a quarter of its peace-time volume, bringing terrible distress amongst the poor people of the town. Hundreds became unemployed and prices of essential foodstuffs, particularly bread, more than doubled.

Yet when peace came in 1815, England was once again supreme on the high seas. She had the largest sea-carrying trade in the world and Liverpool held an immense share of it.

But what of Liverpool itself during these years?

The rich merchant families lived comfortably enough, even through the worst times of the French wars, with their fortnightly assemblies and balls at the Town Hall, and the upper strata of society were sharply divided by money and position. Thomas Creevey, writing in his journal of an evening in Brussels with the Duke of Wellington, described the arrival of Mrs Harvey and Miss Caton, who pretended to be so much grander than they were "to *me*, too, who remembers their grandfather, old Caton, a captain of an Indiaman in Liverpool; their father an adventurer to America, and know their two aunts now at Liverpool—Mrs Woodville and another, who move in about the *third-rate* society of that town!"

For the poor and unemployed of Liverpool, life was vicious and hard. In 1760 the population was 60,000; by 1790 it had more than doubled. To house this vast increase of people who flowed in from Ireland and Wales and all parts of England, rows of sordid little back-to-back houses were quickly thrown up by speculative builders. An American visiting Liverpool in 1780 found the "streets long, narrow, crooked and dirty. . . . We scarcely saw a well-dressed person. . . . The whole complexion of the place was nautical, and so infinitely below all our expectations that naught but the thoughts of the few hours we had to pass here rendered it tolerable."

As the wealthy merchants moved out of their houses in the heart of the town to their new mansions in the suburbs, the poor crowded into them and even the cellars became homes for entire families. By 1790 there were 6,780 cellar dwellers in Liverpool, living about four to a cellar, with no amenities for washing or cooking. Water came from a communal street pump or the nearest river; disease was rife and people drowned their troubles in cheap rum.

There were few facilities for education, apart from a handful of indifferent private schools for the children of tradesmen and the like. The Town Council had appropriated the lands which had originally endowed the John Crosse Grammar School and allowed it to continue in only the meanest and most impoverished way, by the allotment of a parsimonious annual grant.

In 1731 the first workhouse was built, at the corner of College Lane and Hanover Street "to employ the poor . . . and thereby to ease the inhabitants of the great burthen the poor are at present"; but soon more had to be provided, for by 1794 one in every forty inhabitants was in the workhouse and it was estimated that another 10,000 were either living on the parish or being kept alive by private gifts of food.

In 1745 the Royal Infirmary was established, where St George's Hall now stands, and earlier in the century Bryan Blundell, with the co-operation of the Reverend Robert Stythe, founded the Bluecoat Hospital. It began as a day-school for fifty destitute orphans, but before his death, in 1756, Blundell had collected funds, some from his own resources, for the foundation of a permanent boarding-school.

In 1768, at a house in School Lane near Blundell's Bluecoat Hospital, was born Thomas Creevey, whose diaries and letters were to provide such an invaluable and vivid picture of English life during the early years of the nineteenth century. Four years earlier his mother had married William Creevey, the captain of a Liverpool slave ship, but at the time of Thomas's birth he was away at sea and shortly afterwards he died. There is strong evidence that Thomas was Phoebe Creevey's son by the young Earl of Sefton, Lord Molyneux of Croxteth.

When he was twelve or thirteen, Thomas was sent away to Newcome's famous school at Hackney. This would have been far beyond his mother's means and is a further proof that people of some wealth had an interest in him. On leaving school, he went to Cambridge. His mother had married again and there seems to have been no sympathy between her and her son, but Creevey's family advisers were his uncle, John Eaton, and Dr James Currie. Dr Currie belonged to the circle of intellectual Whigs in Liverpool. They liked young Thomas and with their help he went to London to read for the Bar. He was very successful and developed a talent for public speaking. In 1802, when thirty-four he was elected member of Parliament for Thetford and the same year he married a rich widow, several years older than himself, who was a friend of Sheridan, Mrs Fitzherbert and the Prince of Wales, soon to become the Prince Regent.

The Creeveys set up house in Park Place, St James's and Thomas became an important figure in Whig circles. By 1807, however, the Whigs were out of office. In the election of 1812 he and Brougham stood for Liverpool against Canning and Gascoigne. The candidates made speeches to the people of Liverpool throughout the days of the campaign and each evening addressed them from the windows of the houses where they were staying. Canning's host was Sir John Gladstone, who was living in Rodney Street, and one of his listeners was Sir John's small son, William Ewart, at that time three years old.

Canning and Gascoigne won for Liverpool and Brougham and Creevey were out of office. Mrs Creevey was in failing health and the family moved to Brussels for a few years. It was here that Thomas, in letters and journals, described the events before and after Waterloo and his meetings with the Duke of Wellington. Mrs Creevey died in 1818 and the following year Thomas returned to England. By 1820 he was in Parliament again, as member for Appleby, and during the next few years he became increasingly friendly with the Molyneuxs, to whom he often referred as "his own, his *real* family". He lived just into the Victorian age, dying in February 1838.

At the beginning of the Napoleonic Wars another famous person was born in Liverpool: Felicia Hemans, the poetess. She was the daughter of a Liverpool merchant. In 1812, when she was nineteen, she married Captain Hemans, an Irish officer, who left her six years later, after she had borne five sons. Mrs Hemans wrote a great deal of poetry during her short life; although it is probably never read today, it had a great deal of success at the time, and she was held in high regard by many of the leading literary figures of the day, including Wordsworth and Sir Walter Scott. She spent a good deal of her life in Liverpool, but in 1831 she went to live with her brother in Dublin, where, in 1835, she died, at the age of forty-one.

Liverpool in the eighteenth century was essentially commercial, but the arts were not entirely neglected, for it was at this time that the town produced some extremely attractive pottery and porcelain.

Earthenware pottery had been made in England since medieval times. During the sixteenth century it was also imported from Europe, along with stoneware, which is earthenware baked at a very high temperature so that it becomes hard and impervious, and delftware, which is earthenware coated with an opaque lead glaze; both stoneware and delftware were soon being made in English factories.

Porcelain is a stoneware made from china clay. It had been manufactured in China for centuries but it was not until the eighteenth century, when the beautifully decorated dishes, vases and table ware were brought to Europe by the East India merchant ships in large quantities and became so popular and highly prized, that, after much research into the secrets of its manufacture, porcelain factories were opened in Europe. The first was at Meissen, near Dresden, but before long factories had opened in England, notably at Chelsea and Bow.

There is a good deal of controversy about the beginning of the Liverpool potteries. The first delftware is thought to have been made about 1710, when some potters from Southwark moved up to Liverpool and opened a factory, but certain pieces of Liverpool pottery have survived which seem to have been made about the middle of the seventeenth century. These are of tin-glazed earthenware, known as faience.

Alderman Thomas Shaw was making pottery in Liverpool early in the eighteenth century and potters of the later part of the period include Chaffers, Christian, Pennington, Barnes, Harrison and Drinkwater.

About 1750 John Sadler of Liverpool introduced, and may very well have invented, a process of decorating pottery by transfers, the decoration being applied from engraved copper plates by means of sheets of gelatine. This transfer printing eventually took the place of hand-painted decoration and made the work more commercial. Sadler went into partnership with Guy Green and they were so successful that very soon pack-horse trains laden with plain pottery were arriving at Liverpool from other English potteries, including the Wedgwood factory at Burslem, for decoration.

A great deal of this pottery, including jugs, mugs, flower vases, trinket trays and tiles, was exported to America. Decoration, either multi-coloured or blue on white, included flowers, landscapes, figures of sailors and their sweethearts and, after the development of transfer printing, scenes from Hogarth prints, portraits of famous actors and actresses and illustrations from popular books. A speciality of Liverpool potteries was enormous punch bowls for use on ships or for presentation to retiring sea-captains. They were gaily decorated with the name of the ship and pictures of ships, fishes, anchors and anything nautical, in clear bright colours.

By the middle of the century there were about a dozen porcelain factories in Liverpool, some of which had gone over to porcelain from earthenware. The most important porcelain factory, however, was that established in 1756, at Shaw's Brow, by Richard Chaffers, who had come from Worcester. This Liverpool porcelain is very similar to that of Worcester, much of it decorated with Chinese designs of flowers, birds and human figures in bright colours, particularly blue and red, the flowers being outlined in black.

Chaffers died in 1765 and little is known about the factory after this, for by about 1780 the pottery industry in Liverpool was declining and many of the best potters had gone to work in

Staffordshire; but in 1793 the Herculanium factory was opened near the site of the present Herculanium Dock. By 1796 it was employing forty men, women and children who had been brought from Staffordshire and was producing blue-printed earthenware, stoneware jugs, busts, figures and, later, porcelain. The factory changed hands several times and was finally closed in 1841, when it was demolished to make way for the dock. Unlike most Liverpool pottery, Herculanium ware was marked, one of the marks being the liver bird surrounded by a floral scroll.

Examples of Liverpool delftware and porcelain are to be found in the Liverpool Museum and also at the Victoria and Albert Museum and the British Museum in London.

Another notable product of Liverpool was watches. By early in the eighteenth century the town had become famous for excellent watches and by 1800 the industry was employing nearly 2,000 craftsmen, who were producing about 150 watches a week, some for export to America and a few even to Geneva, which was to become so noted for its watch-making industry.

9. COTTON

At the end of the American War of Independence, many merchants in Liverpool feared that France would capture the American market. At first France did send produce to America, but she could not supply the manufactured goods—the cotton and woollen cloth, ironware and earthenware—which America needed, and Liverpool was soon in business again. Between 1783 and 1793 the port was busier than it had ever been and the slave trade was revived. Moreover, Liverpool recovered her ship-building industry. The American colonies had been taking an increasing share of this business but now Liverpool shipwrights began building with timber imported from Canada.

In 1785 the port had two dry docks and three wet docks—the Old Dock, the Salthouse and St George's Docks. Work now began on two more wet docks, the King's Dock, opened in 1786, and the Queen's Dock, completed in 1796. This meant that the shipyards had to be moved and eventually the docks were so extensive that the ship-building industry moved to the Birkenhead side of the river.

By 1800 the great days of ship-building were over in Liverpool, the watchmaking industry had dwindled through American and Swiss competition and most of the potters had moved to Staffordshire. The businessmen of Liverpool were not manufacturers. They were ship-owners, handlers and transporters of goods and commodities; and they were anxious to ensure that as much as possible of England's manufacturers, particularly those of Manchester, were transported in Liverpool ships.

William Pitt the Younger had become Prime Minister of

England in 1783, at the age of twenty-five, and after concluding the peace treaties with America and France, he made many financial reforms in England, including the reduction of import duties, so that smuggling was no longer worthwhile and smugglers were put out of business. The smuggling on the Isle of Man had already been suppressed some years earlier, when the descendants of the Derby family had surrendered the island to the Crown, for a payment of £70,000; and in 1785, much to Liverpool's advantage, free trade was established between Ireland and England, so that Irish linen now came in increasing quantities through Liverpool, in exchange for coal, textiles, tea and hardware.

With the increasing demands of the abolitionists, the wisest Liverpool merchants, seeing that the end of the slave trade was inevitable, began to seek a fresh outlet for their enterprise and found the answer in cotton.

It was as early as June 1757, shortly after the outbreak of the Seven Years War, that an advertisement appeared in the *Liverpool Chronicle and Marine Gazetteer*: "To be sold by auction at the Merchants' Coffee House, on Thursday, the 16th inst. at one o'clock precisely 28 bags of Jamaica cotton in four lots. Samples to be seen with R. Robinson, Broker."

This announcement was the beginning of the Liverpool cotton market. As we have seen, small parcels of cotton had been arriving in Liverpool, along with the cargoes of sugar, rum and tobacco, during the previous fifty years, but until this time the import of cotton had been desultory. Now there was an increasing demand for it and Liverpool ship-owners and brokers were issuing definite instructions to their captains for its purchase. Trade figures show that in 1720, 1,972,805 pounds of cotton were coming into the country. By 1764 the amount had doubled. In 1784 11,000,000 pounds of cotton were imported into Great Britain but in 1785 the figure had risen to over 18,000,000 and in 1786 it was 19,500,000 pounds. Most of this came from the West Indies, though 5,000,000 pounds were from Turkey and Cyprus. Very little as yet was arriving from the United States of America.

The cotton-buying merchants were all in and around Manchester, close to the concentration of spinners and weavers in south-east Lancashire, who still worked in their own cottages. This hand work was slow; it took ten spinners to keep one weaver supplied with yarn, but the spinners liked the long-staple West Indian cotton, which was considered to be the finest obtainable, and cotton cloth was becoming increasingly popular.

Richard Robinson had a counting house in the High Street. Within the next few years more merchants and brokers, most of whom lived over their counting houses in Water Street, Dale Street, Castle Street, Moor Street and High Street, began buying cotton from the West Indies. At first they used to meet and exchange news and business in the open air at the end of Castle Street or in the neighbouring coffee houses. They were offered accommodation in the Exchange, but these elegantly dressed merchants, with their tricorn hats over their small wigs, their knee breeches, silk stockings and buckled shoes, their knee-length coats and long waistcoats, frilled shirts and high neckcloths, seem to have preferred to do their business and conduct their auctions in the open air.

Inventions were being patented which would speed up the processes of spinning and weaving and absorb vastly more quantities of cotton. In 1764 James Hargreaves, a weaver living near Blackburn, invented a spinning machine which he named after his wife Jenny. The first Spinning Jenny, by the operation of a hand-wheel, turned eight spindles simultaneously and produced excellent weft threads. Hargreaves installed several in his home, but other spinners, suspicious of the new device, broke into his house and smashed them. It made little difference to the ultimate development of spinning machines, however, and by 1769 Richard Arkwright had invented a machine which produced a thread of the right firmness for a warp.

In 1774 Samuel Crompton's "mule" was producing yarn faster than the weaver could use it, but within a few years a fly shuttle had been invented which doubled the weaver's output; and in 1785 Cartwright perfected the power loom, which enabled one man to weave as much as ten men had previously achieved in the same time.

By this time America was independent. Until 1776 the southern states had grown cotton in relatively small quantities for their own use, but after the peace treaty planters quickly turned their attention to cotton cultivation as a commercial crop for the Lancashire cotton industry.

The first plantings on a commercial scale were in the coastal regions of the southern Atlantic states. Here soil and climate were excellent and there were port facilities at Charleston, Savannah and Norfolk, Virginia, well situated for Liverpool. Moreover, these states already had a large Negro population to work the plantations, follow the mule-drawn ploughs, hoe and gather the harvest. Most were slaves, but some were by now free men. The slaves had not, for the most part, been transported directly by the Liverpool slavers, for the Liverpool men had traded mainly with the West Indies. A few captains who had not been able to sell all their slaves in the islands had occasionally sailed up the coast to Georgia, the Carolinas and Maryland and disposed of them easily enough, but many of the American planters had carried on a slave trade of their own, operating between Rhode Island, New Providence and the Gold Coast. In 1773, the year of the Boston Tea Party which began the War of Independence, 4,500 Negroes had been shipped to Charleston, selling at an average price of £50.

In 1784 the United States shipped 1,800 pounds of cotton to Liverpool and by 1789 the figure had risen to 126,300 pounds. At the same time, Americans managed to smuggle copies of the new Lancashire machinery into the United States and began a cotton industry of their own. But they had millions of acres of virgin lands in the south which were ideal for cotton cultivation and in 1803 Napoleon sold to the United States the French colony of Lousiana, which was to become the greatest cotton-producing country in the world.

America was soon sending increasingly large quantities of raw cotton to Liverpool and by now the Industrial Revolution had dawned. James Watt had invented the steam engine and steam engines were installed in the cotton and woollen mills of Yorkshire and Lancashire. The days of the cottage spinners and weavers were ending. Steam-driven machinery meant factories, and the cottagers had to move to the towns where they were being built.

In Liverpool the cotton brokers were kept busy and by 1800, although we were in the midst of the Napoleonic Wars, American cotton imports had risen to nearly 18 million pounds.

In 1795 the Exchange and Town Hall suffered a disastrous fire and much of the interior had to be rebuilt, but the cotton merchants still transacted their business in front of it, at the top of Castle Street, to the increasing annoyance of other people and the shopkeepers:

"When the traffic was unusually heavy the scene would be one of colourful animation. A hopeless jam of bobbing sedan-chairs (which were just going out), horse-drawn cabs (which were just coming in), with their whip-flicking, tongue-clicking cabbies; elegant turnouts, horsemen, urchins, beggars, curious sightseers, sailors, hawkers (successors to the chapmen), messengers and counting-house clerks, all mixed up on the outskirts of the central knot of brokers, merchants, bankers and dealers, probably a little excited, putting through a record weight of business for their 'constituents' (as they called their clients at the time), some of whom would undoubtedly be on the fringe of the crowd, swelling the numbers; all of them treading a soft carpet of well stamped-down horse manure . . . and when it rained, as rain it undoubtedly would, the English weather being no kinder then than now, the helter-skelter rush to get the best positions in the shop doorways would stir up the already animated scene into one of colourful chaos."[1]

In 1803 a New Exchange was opened at the back of the Town Hall, where the dealers were transferred to do their business, yet they still preferred to deal on the "flags" which formed the courtyard of the new building. Here the different brokers took up their stands. They kept a record of their transactions and at

[1] "A Short History of the Liverpool Cotton Market", W. F. Machin, *Liverpool Raw Cotton Annual*, 1957.

the end of the day returned to their offices to make out the contracts.

The cotton market was divided into two sections: the buying brokers who bought the cotton on a commission basis for the Manchester spinners, thus saving them the long, awkward journey from Manchester, and the selling brokers who imported the cotton and sold it to the buying brokers.

During the first quarter of the nineteenth century, the import of American cotton rose from 17·7 million pounds to 124·3 million pounds. In addition, by 1823 the first imports of Sudanese and Egyptian cotton arrived in Liverpool, for Mohammed Ali had recently introduced its cultivation there.

With this enormous increase of imports, the buying brokers in Liverpool, instead of inspecting the entire mass of cotton put up for auction in the salesrooms of the selling brokers, bought it "by sample", for they had become extremely knowledgeable about cotton and could judge its quality quickly and accurately.

The biggest problem now facing the merchants was how to convey the raw cotton quickly to Manchester and the manufactured goods back to Liverpool, for inland transport was still very difficult. By 1820 a thousand tons of freight were being carried on the canals each day between the two centres, at a cost of fifteen shillings a ton, but there were still interminable delays at the locks, and when the waterways were frozen the dealers had to cart it by road, at double the cost, in order to keep the cotton moving and the mills in steady production.

In 1770 there were two coaches a day running between Manchester and Liverpool, but by 1800 seventy coaches a week were in service and the inns round Castle Street, Dale Street and Water Street all prospered, particularly the *Talbot* in Water Street.

The Manchester buyers would arrive in Liverpool by coach, make their purchases and send them back by the waterways or by carts and pack-horses. In 1788 a record of seventy pack-horses were despatched to Manchester from one Liverpool inn in a single day.

By 1825 there were twenty-two regular coaches running each day and another seven were available when needed, which together could carry 688 people. There were a number of rival companies engaged in the coaching business and there was fierce competition between them to provide the quickest service. During the 1770s the thirty-five-mile journey took about twelve hours. In 1773, for example, the Diligence coach, which left Manchester at six a.m., advertised breakfast at Irlam, dinner at Warrington, tea at Prescott and arrival at Liverpool by nightfall. By the early 1820s, when the roads had improved and also the design of the coaches, the time had been cut to three hours. This, allowing for three changes of horses, was an average speed of twelve miles an hour.

Yet the road from Manchester to Liverpool was still primitive and there were many accidents through coaches overturning. In 1825 a correspondent in the *Manchester Guardian* complained that "the soft part [of the road] is uneven, the substance of it in many places quite worn through, and the pavement is infamous. It is constantly the subject of complaint with the great 'tide of human existence' which is flowing in a ceaseless current between these two populous cities, and it is observed with astonishment by all strangers who come from other parts of the Kingdom . . . this road . . . remains almost in the same state it was in twenty years ago, as circuitous, crooked, and probably as rough."

The canal companies maintained and improved their waterways, built warehouses and did everything they could to encourage users, but they were still subject to hazards of the weather and there were constant complaints of delays by winds and tides, long waits in the locks, summer droughts, flooding and ice in winter, a shortage of barges and high rates.

By 1825 the Stockton–Darlington coal-carrying steam locomotive railway was in operation and two years later Stephenson's *Rocket* won the Rainhill trials, reaching a speed of thirty-five miles an hour.

Passenger railways had become a possibility, but when the first suggestion of building a railway between Liverpool and

Manchester was made, there was an outburst of protest, not only from the Turnpike Trusts, who were still responsible for the maintenance of roads, and the canal companies, whose interests would be seriously affected, but by the owners of the land through which the railway must pass and by many members of the general public who were mortally afraid of the new steam engine. Elderly gentlemen would not dare to cross the railway, for fear of being run down, they said. Hunting would be ruined. Cows would not graze within sight of the locomotives. Women would miscarry at the sight of the smoking engines. Farmhouses would be burned down by sparks, and farmlands destroyed. Horses would become extinct, for there would be no further use for them, and what would then become of all the oats farmers grew?

There were angry debates in Parliament and Thomas Creevey was one of the bitterest opponents, acting in the interests of his friends Lord Sefton and Lord Derby.

"Well—this devil of a railway is strangled at last," he wrote to his stepdaughter in May 1825. "I was sure that yesterday's division had put him on his last legs, and today we had a clear majority in the Committee in our favour, and the promoters of the Bill withdrew it, and took their leave of us. . . . We had to fight this long battle against an almost universal prejudice to start with—interested shareholders and perfidious Whigs, several of whom affected to oppose us upon *conscientious* scruples. Sefton's ecstasies are *beyond*, and he is pleased to say it has been all my doing; so it's all mighty well."

Yet the age of steam had arrived. The first steamboat had been seen in the Mersey in 1815 and in 1819 the first to cross the Atlantic reached Liverpool on its way from New York to St Petersburg. When it was at last realized that the journey from Liverpool to Manchester—which was still taking anything up to thirty-six hours by water, at a charge of fifteen shillings a ton —could be accomplished by rail in under three hours, with a charge of ten shillings a ton for freight, supporters for the railway gradually made progress and at last, with persuasion from the Liverpool member, William Huskisson, Parliament gave its assent. The Enabling Act of 1826 permitted a railway to be built. Yet the question of using a steam locomotive was still not settled, for many people even yet thought it would be safer for the coaches to be pulled along the railway by horses and deplored the high speeds claimed for the locomotive.

An anonymous reviewer in the *Quarterly Review* for March, 1825, obviously expected the very worst to happen, when he wrote: "It is certainly some consolation to those who are to be whirled at the rate of eighteen or twenty miles an hour, by means of a high pressure engine, to be told that they are in no danger of being seasick while on shore; that they are not to be scalded to death nor drowned by the bursting of the boiler; and that they need not mind being shot by the scattered fragments, or dashed in pieces by the flying off, or the breaking of a wheel."

The project for the building of the railway took shape. When Stephenson was making his preliminary survey of the route, he and his assistants were stoned and the situation grew so serious that, in the end, they had to work after dark, by the light of lanterns. At one point Stephenson was dismissed and the Rennie brothers were put in charge, but eventually Stephenson was back in office and, with his army of labourers, many of whom were Irishmen, built the railway. He attended to every detail himself, including the problem of draining Chat Moss and excavating the tunnel under Liverpool, which was dug by candle-light.

Opening day was on 15th September, 1830. Grandstands were erected in Liverpool and there were at least 50,000 spectators. Amongst the distinguished guests who were invited to ride on the first passenger-railway journey were the Prime Minister, the Duke of Wellington, Prince Esterhazy, the Austrian Ambassador, the Marquess of Salisbury, Sir Robert Peel, a host of earls, viscounts, peers and bishops, as well as distinguished engineers and members of Parliament, including William Huskisson.

With flags flying and bands playing, eight trains assembled, one driven by Stephenson, on the south line, drawing three carriages, the other seven on the north line, hauling four or five carriages each, all full of guests.

During the seventeen miles between Liverpool and Parkside, the trains reached a speed of between fourteen and twenty-four miles an hour, and at Parkside all engines stopped to take on water. Though they had been warned not to alight, several people, including Huskisson, travelling on the south line, climbed down and walked along the track at Parkside. It seemed to be clear, but suddenly one of the north line trains appeared. Everyone except Huskisson jumped to safety. He tried to climb into one of the carriages but fell back. The driver could not stop in time and the wheels of the engine and several of the carriages ran over his thigh and leg. He was taken as

Opening the railway, 1830

quickly as possible to Eccles but his injuries were terrible and a few hours later he died.

It was a sad beginning for the venture, but within a few months it had proved itself. Creevey took a lot of convincing. Describing a journey at twenty-three miles an hour, he wrote: ". . . the quickest motion is to me *frightful*: it is really flying,

and it is impossible to divest yourself of the notion of instant death to all upon the least accident happening. It gave me a headache which has not left me yet. Sefton is convinced that some damnable thing must come of it; but he and I seem more struck with such apprehension than others. . . ." And that was just as well, for the same week a regular passenger service began between Liverpool and Manchester, three trains a day carrying about 130 passengers, at a charge of seven shillings, and the journey taking under two hours. Then two trains a day of second-class carriages were put into service, with places at four shillings.

The coach fare had been twelve shillings for an inside seat and seven shillings for outside and the trip, except for the "fliers", took four and a half hours.

The coaches reduced their fares but were unable to compete. By the end of the year a thousand passengers were travelling by rail between Liverpool and Manchester every day; passenger fares had been reduced, and trains had begun to carry the mail and also freight. The canals hastily reduced their freight charges for cotton from fifteen to ten shillings a ton, but it was too late. The railway had won.

The improved connection was a boon to the Liverpool cotton brokers. All cotton buying was now concentrated in Liverpool and by 1832 the port had become the biggest importing raw cotton market in the world.

10. AND STILL MORE COTTON

At the beginning of the nineteenth century, while the merchants prospered and moved from their counting houses to magnificent country mansions in the surrounding countryside, the poor people of Liverpool—as in most other rapidly expanding commercial and industrial towns, particularly in the north, during the early years of the industrial revolution—were underpaid, uneducated, overworked, underfed and disease-ridden. Many were on the verge of starvation and most lived in a state of degrading squalor.

It was not only the workhouses of Liverpool which were full. The prisons, too, were always crowded, for transportation to America had ceased after 1776 and it was several years before the Australian penal settlements were founded. The principal prison, both for felons and debtors, was still the Tower at the bottom of Water Street. It had seven underground dungeons, each about six feet square, with only holes in the doors for light and ventilation, and prisoners were lodged here three to a dungeon. There was another somewhat larger room, where about twelve men and women were herded together. Debtors were kept in one of the towers. The destitute were provided with straw; those who had a little money left could share a bed for two at a charge of a shilling a week. A minimum of food was supplied by charity and the debtors were allowed to beg from passers-by.

On the north side of the St George's Dock was another prison, which was said to be "damp and offensive" and "totally dark and unventilated", but this was replaced, in 1804, by a new "house of correction", or "bridewell", in Chapel Street.

For vagrants and "disorderly people" there was also a house of correction on Brownlow Hill by the workhouse.

With the prison reforming movement of John Howard, who visited Liverpool prisons in the course of his investigations, a new prison was built in Great Howard Street and the houses of correction were demolished; by 1819 the Tower had also been pulled down and Water Street widened.

Apart from this, the Town Council did little to help the poor of Liverpool, but spent a great deal of money on improving the town itself. When the Town Hall was rebuilt after the fire of 1795, all the sleazy alleys and courts behind it were cleared away to make room for the New Exchange building. The Council also built a monument to Lord Nelson, though poor Emma Hamilton, who had been born in Wirral and spoke all her life with a strong Liverpool accent, was now living in Calais in dire poverty and could well have done with some of the money. The Old Dock at the other end of Castle Street was filled in and a fine new Customs House built.

Castle Street, Dale Street and Water Street were all widened and improved, yet the Council lacked real vision in the replanning of their town and made little provision for parks and open spaces. Even the Ladies' Walks had disappeared by now. On one houses had been built and the other had disappeared when the Leeds and Liverpool canal had been cut. There were, however, the bowling greens on Mount Pleasant, and where the Adelphi Hotel now stands were the Ranelagh Gardens, a smaller version of the Ranelagh Pleasure Gardens at Chelsea, with firework displays, dancing and music in the evenings.

The Theatre Royal in Williamson Square, which had been opened in 1762, was enlarged in 1803, but there was little cultivation of the arts, apart from a music festival held every three years. It had begun in 1784, when Liverpool society flocked to hear Handel's oratorios and were afterwards regaled with a banquet and ball at the Town Hall. Most people were content to divert themselves with dog-fighting, cock-fighting and bull-baiting, and there were a prodigious number of taverns in the town where they could buy cheap spirits.

The humanitarian movements which were gradually to improve the lot of the industrial poor began with the evangel-cal preaching of the Wesleys and the religious revival, in all the denominations, which soon followed. Charles Wesley visited Liverpool on several occasions and a great number of new churches were built in the town about this time, both Anglican and Roman Catholic as well as Nonconformist, and many charitable organizations and new schools were founded.

The old grammar school had been for the sons of freemen, but having been robbed of most of its original endowment it had become so impoverished that few freemen availed themselves of the opportunity. By the beginning of the century it was housed in a wing of the Bluecoat School and when the last grammar school master died, in 1802, it was allowed to become extinct. In its place the Council founded two free elementary schools, the North and South Corporation schools.

The Sunday school movement had been founded by Robert Raikes at Gloucester, in 1780. His first school was intended for the very poor children working in the factories, who had no time during the week to attend a school, even if there were one available. He opened many more and they attracted large numbers of children and also their parents, who would walk for miles to attend them, carrying their Sunday dinners with them, and spend all day learning reading, writing and arithmetic and receiving religious instruction. Similar schools were launched in Liverpool, the children arriving at one o'clock every Sunday and staying "until evening comes on".

By 1789 the Moorfields Charity School had been founded, for 200 boys and 120 girls, who paid a penny a week, and early in the nineteenth century the Church of England National Society schools and the non-sectarian schools of the British and Foreign Schools Society, which were appearing all over the country, were being established in Liverpool.

Yet these schools provided for only a very small percentage of children and in 1818, when the population of England and Wales was about 12,000,000, it was estimated that probably no more than 40,000 children were passing through the Charity

Schools. By 1835 little more than half the children of Liverpool were receiving any schooling at all.

In 1817 William Roscoe, one of Liverpool's most distinguished citizens, founded the Royal Institution. William Roscoe was outstanding because, in a town given over almost exclusively to commerce and money-making, he strove to foster an interest in the arts. Born in 1753, the son of an innkeeper, he had no formal education after the age of twelve but taught himself Latin, French and Italian and read a great deal of medieval Italian history.

William Roscoe

He dreamed of endowing Liverpool with all the graces of fifteenth-century Florence, and in this he showed a remarkable vision, for despite the gracious buildings that were going up in Rodney Street, Abercromby Square and Falkner Square, there could not have been a more stark contrast between Renaissance Florence and the sordid, squalid port area. Roscoe helped to promote the Athenaeum library in 1799, the Botanic Gardens in 1802, the Lyceum in 1803, the Academy of Art in 1810, the Literary and Philosophical Society in 1812, and, in 1817, the Royal Institution, which he hoped might become the centre of what little there was of Liverpool's intellectual and artistic life.

In 1825 the Mechanics' School of Arts, later renamed the Mechanics' Institution, provided evening classes for artisans, and in 1835 a day school was added, which was to become the Liverpool Institute Boys' and Girls' High Schools. In 1834 a medical school had been founded, in association with the Liverpool Royal Infirmary, and many years later, in 1881, a University College. This college was at first part of the federal Victoria University, comprising Owens College, Manchester and the Yorkshire College at Leeds, but in 1903 it was granted independent status as the University of Liverpool.

Until the Municipal Reform Act of 1835, the Town Council of Liverpool, composed of forty-one freemen, had undertaken the building of the docks, the erection of public buildings and churches and the widening of streets, the money for which came from its large income, derived from dock dues, town dues, market dues and other ancient rights, and nothing had been charged to the rates. Yet the admission of freemen by purchase was still forbidden, which meant that there were now many rich merchants and important citizens in the town, such as William Roscoe, who had no hope of a seat on the Council. This meant that they were not allowed to vote for the Mayor nor had they a vote in Parliamentary elections.

The Common Council still took no responsibility for the appalling slum conditions in the older part of the town nor for the well-being of the increasing number of unskilled workers who were needed as casual labourers, with no regular wage, to man the docks. The Council considered its duties were merely to maintain the interests of the small body of freemen, and the time was obviously ripe for a radical change.

In 1835 the municipal corporation, which had existed for over 450 years, was abolished and nearly all the ancient and outmoded privileges of the freemen, which included exemption from paying town dues on merchandise and shipping, were withdrawn. In place of the old Common Council, a freely elected Council was established, which, for the next six years, was predominantly Whig.

The task of cleaning up the town, to which the new Council had committed itself, was extremely difficult, for the slums round the docks were spreading and deteriorating every year. As at the Port of London, there were abundant opportunities for river pirates, night plunderers, mudlarks and receivers and in Liverpool at least 1,200 regular thieves were under the age of fifteen.

The police force was reorganized and its numbers doubled, in a drive aimed not only at catching the criminals but at trying to prevent crime and other vices.

The overcrowding in the slums was made worse during the terrible Irish potato famine of 1845-6. In Ireland two million of the eight million population died of starvation and of the survivors, thousands flocked to Liverpool. During the first three months of 1846 more than 90,000 arrived, utterly destitute, and between July 1847 and July 1848 another 300,000 landed. Many later emigrated to America but enough remained in Liverpool to form an Irish quarter, where they lived in desperate poverty.

The Council appointed a building surveyor and the houses which were structurally dangerous were pulled down, though no steps were taken as yet to rehouse the dispossessed occupants. To ameliorate the insanitary conditions of the remaining houses, public wash-houses were built and building regulations were imposed on all new houses.

The new Whig Council reorganized the North and South Corporation schools but trouble at once arose over the question of religious education. The Irish Catholics did not want their children taught according to the faith of the Church of England. The non-Catholics insisted that the Protestant religion should be taught. The Whigs suggested a compromise teaching of the essentials of Christianity, but this seemed to please no one and the argument was so bitter on both sides that in the next election the Whigs lost their power and the Council became predominantly Conservative.

The town's civic dignity was enhanced by the building of the beautiful St George's Hall between 1838 and 1854, which was intended both as a concert hall and assize court. Yet conditions round the docks were as bad as ever. In 1843 Dr William Duncan, a lecturer at the School of Medicine attached to the Infirmary, published an account of the living conditions in the Liverpool slums which at last shocked the prosperous early

St George's Hall, 1834

Victorians of Liverpool into some positive action. Dr Duncan reported that only in the middle and upper class residential areas of the town were there any sewers. He described conditions in the lodging houses where, as in London, casual visitors would be herded sixteen or seventeen to a room or in the cellars, on piles of straw. The density of the population in these Liverpool slums was 100,000 to a square mile, higher than anywhere else in the country; and one in twenty-five people suffered every year from a contagious fever, such as typhoid or cholera, which in most cases was fatal.

The Council obtained powers to make itself responsible for the laying of sewers in the town and for inspecting lodging houses, though there were many who protested that the inspection of the rooming houses was a threat to personal liberty. Stricter building regulations were imposed and factories were obliged to consume their own smoke.

In 1846 Dr Duncan was appointed the town's medical officer and a vigorous campaign was waged against insanitary dwellings. More than 14,000 inhabited cellars were visited and in nearly 6,000 there were found to be stagnant pools of water under the floors. More than 5,000 were condemned and the inhabitants removed, and many slum houses were demolished.

Water had been brought to the town by two rival companies, one of which obtained supplies from wells at Bootle, the other from wells at Toxteth Park; but it was far from being a continuous supply, for it was turned on for only a quarter of an hour or, at the most, half an hour at a time, on alternate days. With a single standpipe serving a whole courtyard of perhaps a hundred families, people had to line up with jugs and buckets, and those who missed their turn had to wait another two days for fresh water.

The Town Council bought up the two companies and built reservoirs at Rivington, north of Bolton, so that the town was at last able to enjoy a continuous supply of water, but as the population continued to increase they used so much that very soon the Rivington reservoirs were not large enough. In 1880, therefore, Lake Vyrnwy was created in the heart of the Welsh mountains, to supply Liverpool, by means of vast pipes, with an abundant supply of fresh water.

In 1852 the Liverpool Public Library was opened, one of the first in the country. The original library building was in Duke Street, but in 1860 it moved to the present building, which was presented to the town by Sir William Brown. He also presented the Museum building in which were housed the thirteenth Earl of Derby's natural history collection, presented in 1851, and the Joseph Mayer collection of antiquities, bequeathed a few years later.

In 1873, during his term of office as Mayor, Sir Andrew Barclay Walker presented the splendid Walker Art Gallery, built, like the St George's Hall, in the classical style, with a magnificent pillared portico. Today, amongst the gallery's treasures, is the finest collection of Pre-Raphaelite paintings in the country.

In 1879 the Council added a large, circular reading room to the library, in honour of Sir James Picton, and within the next few years the 269 acres of Sefton Park were rescued from what remained of the ancient Toxteth Park and several other municipal parks and playgrounds were formed.

After the Elementary Education Act of 1870 ensured that every child in the country should receive at least an elementary education, the Liverpool School Board built many more schools, to supplement the few existing ones, and the Liverpool Council of Education provided good opportunities for scholarships to places of higher education. Facilities for technical and science training were provided and colleges for art and teacher-training established, while the Technical College was built between 1897 and 1901.

Although a few cottages had been built to replace the condemned tenements, it was not until 1885 that the problem of housing was seriously considered. That year Victoria Square was built, and by the end of the century the Council had provided accommodation for 700 families. 1897 saw the arrival of electric trams and this first rapid transport through the town made it possible for council houses to be built away from the site of the old slums. The pace of demolition and reconstruction quickened and by 1907 more than 2,000 corporation houses had been built.

In 1800 the population of Liverpool was 77,078. By 1851 it was 376,065, and by 1901 the figure had reached 684,047, for people had by this time spread into the neighbouring townships, which were gradually absorbed into the main town. The boundary of Liverpool was first extended in 1835, taking in the northern part of Toxteth Park, the townships of Kirkdale and Everton and a part of West Derby, but Bootle was granted a separate charter in 1868.

When the steam ferry connected the two banks of the Mersey in 1817, many Liverpool inhabitants moved to the Cheshire side of the river, creating the boroughs of Birkenhead and Wallasey; Birkenhead was incorporated with Liverpool in 1877 and Wallasey in 1910. In 1895 Walton and Wavertree, most of the remainder of West Derby and the southern half of Toxteth were added to Liverpool; in 1902 Garston, in 1905 Fazakerley, in 1913 Allerton, Childwall, Little Woolton and Much Woolton, in 1928 the remainder of West Derby and Croxteth and in 1932 Speke, with its beautiful Tudor manor house, Speke Hall, which is probably the oldest home in Liverpool. For generations the Norreys family lived at Speke and their history is a part not only of Liverpool's story but of England's, for they were involved in many wars and national events. Eventually the manor came by marriage to the Beauclerk family, descendants of the Duke of St Albans, who was Charles II's son by Nell Gwynne. They were a spendthrift lot and by the end of the eighteenth century much of the ancient grandeur of Speke had departed. They sold it to Richard Watt, a merchant who had made his fortune in the West Indies, and his descendants continued to live there until the last of the line died in 1921. Speke Hall is an outstanding example of Tudor domestic architecture and is now the property of the National Trust, but the Liverpool Corporation has leased it from them for 99 years.

In 1850 the Roman Catholic Church made Liverpool the

seat of a diocese and later an archbishopric, but it had to wait
for more than a hundred years before the cathedral was built.

In 1880 a royal charter granted Liverpool the status of a city.
It became the seat of a new diocese but, like the Catholics, the
Anglicans had to wait until the present century before their
cathedral was built.

As a final honour to the city, in 1893 Queen Victoria
conferred on Liverpool's chief officer the title of Lord Mayor.

These were years of astonishing progress and prosperity for
Liverpool. By the end of the Napoleonic Wars England had
changed from a country which was predominantly agricultural
and still self-sufficient in essential requirements to a great manufacturing centre; and the markets for her goods were assured by
the growing needs of the pioneers of her Empire. The manufacturing cities of the Midlands and the north had made
England the workshop of the world.

Until about 1870 Europe was bedevilled by political troubles
which were an aftermath of the French Revolution, while the
United States, torn by its own civil war during the 1860s, was
still pioneering its vast territories.

England had a clear field. For a few decades she was the
supreme industrial, commercial and colonial power in the
world and Liverpool handled a third of her export trade and a
quarter of her imports. In 1835 Liverpool shipping amounted
to 1,768,426 tons. By 1870 it had risen to 5,728,504 tons. By the
end of the century, although Europe and America were now
competing in both the industrial and mercantile fields, Liverpool's tonnage had risen to close on sixteen millions and the
port had become one of the most important in the world,
owning one-third of Britain's shipping and one-seventh of the
registered shipping of the entire world.

In 1840, Samuel Cunard obtained from the Admiralty the
contract for the transatlantic post, which was worth £60,000 a
year. He pioneered the service between Great Britain, Canada
and the United States with wooden paddle-steamers. His first
steamer, *Britannia*, left Liverpool on 4th July, 1840, and reached
Boston, Massachusetts fourteen days and eight hours later. The

An early Cunard paddle-steamer

Cunard company maintained a regular mail service across the Atlantic, which became increasingly quick and more frequent, and by 1862 the company was making a weekly crossing, the record speed in the last of the Cunard paddle-steamers, the *Scotia*, being eight days and twenty-two hours from New York to Liverpool.

Yet for many years to come, cotton still crossed the Atlantic in the old windjammers. Brokers in Liverpool were never certain when supplies were arriving, for a ship would sometimes wait for weeks at an American port, till it had a full cargo. The Atlantic crossing took anything from six to eight weeks, according to the weather, and there was always the risk of the vessel foundering, with a total loss.

With the inauguration of the Cunard service, American growers would rush their samples by land to New York and put them on the mail boats. This meant that they reached Liverpool, and dealers would make their purchases by sample, several weeks before they received the bulk consignments.

The price of cotton, like that of other commodities, varied with supply and demand. If the price fell after the broker had contracted his purchase, because, for example, of an exceptionally good harvest, he was faced with a loss. If he had bought at a low price and the figure had risen by the time he had taken possession of it at the Liverpool docks and was in a position to sell it, he made a handsome profit.

This situation led to speculative dealing, cotton being sold on the high seas and the buyer gambling on its price when it arrived in Liverpool.

In 1841 the ninety cotton firms in the town formed themselves into the *Liverpool Cotton Brokers Association*, still transacting their business on the "flags" outside the Exchange and finding out as much as they could of the state of the cotton fields and possible dates of arrival of consignments.

For the next few years the price of cotton remained fairly stable and everyone prospered. Trouble began with the outbreak of the American Civil War in 1861. At first supplies were not greatly affected, but by 1862, as the Confederacy began to lose the Atlantic ports, the shortage grew serious. On Merseyside, thirty or forty special ships, each of about 300 tons, were built for blockade-running and were very successful, for only a few were lost, but when Charleston and Wilmington fell, the South had no ports left, either on the Atlantic or the Gulf of Mexico. In 1861 the United States had sent 1,841,600 bales of cotton to Liverpool but in 1862 only 71,766 were shipped, at a frightful risk, through the blockade. Prices rose from $12\frac{1}{2}d$. a pound in 1861 to $22\frac{3}{4}d$. in 1863 and $31\frac{1}{2}d$. in 1864.

Liverpool brokers obtained supplies from other sources. Egyptian cotton was popular. The shortage put the Egyptian industry on its feet and it benefited permanently. Supplies were drawn from Turkey and the Far East. West Indian plantations revived and cultivation was developed in Brazil. Cotton was also imported from India, but Manchester could not send back enough manufactured cotton for India's demands and India, from this time, increased her own manufactures.

Rising prices meant prosperous times for the Liverpool brokers, but the grave shortage which persisted, despite these alternative sources of supply, meant that the cotton industry as a whole suffered terribly. In Manchester, mills were closing and by the end of 1862 a million cotton workers were out of work. By 1866 and the end of the war, the cotton famine had caused three hundred mills to close. There were a thousand bankruptcies in Manchester and in Liverpool more than a hundred cotton firms and two banks had failed.

After 1866 supplies came in again, but the price of cotton now began to drop steadily and it was the turn of the brokers to suffer.

It was in this year, however, that the first Atlantic cable was laid. News could reach Liverpool from the cotton fields more quickly than ever. At this point, with the Liverpool cotton market in dire distress, one of its members, John Rew, devised an ingenious method of protection against possible losses through declining prices.

Let us suppose a broker had agreed to supply a Manchester spinner with a thousand pounds of cotton. The customer agreed to buy it at the price it would be when it reached Liverpool. If the broker had bought by sample at a shilling a pound and by the time it reached Liverpool the price had dropped to ten-pence a pound, he was faced with a loss of twopence a pound. At the same time as he placed his order in America, however, he also sold on the Exchange a thousand pounds of cotton at a shilling a pound, for delivery five or six weeks later, on arrival. He sold his cotton to the Manchester spinner at tenpence a pound, but also bought a thousand pounds at tenpence a pound to fulfil his second deal. He thereby made two transactions. He bought a thousand pounds of cotton at a shilling and sold them at tenpence. He bought a thousand at tenpence and sold them at a shilling. His losses on the first deal were balanced by his profits on the second.

This method of business, known as the "futures" market, invented in Liverpool, was later adopted by the great London exchanges, such as the Baltic and the Metal Exchange, and is still in use.

The Liverpool cotton market revived. In 1882 the Brokers Association was replaced by the Liverpool Cotton Association. Dealings still took place in the open air and trading was so fast, noisy and exciting that it became a popular show for visitors. The merchants, well aware that they were providing good entertainment, took great pride in their appearance and were known as the best dressed businessmen outside the City of London.

Even the "futures" market remained outside, the brokers forming themselves into a ring and calling their bids and acceptances across it. With the arrival of the telephone in the 1880s and the general speeding up of marketing and rapid reporting of news and prices, this open-air dealing became impractical. In 1896 the "futures" market moved into Brown's Buildings, overlooking the "flags", and merchants concerned in the day-to-day selling of cotton moved to offices close by.

During the last years of the century, business in cotton increased so much that, in 1903, the Liverpool Cotton Exchange was built. The main Exchange Room had a central cotton ring, surrounded by four tiers of seats, for the traders in the "futures" market, and in the rest of the building were the offices and sale rooms of the member firms, where most of the business in cotton was conducted.

These years marked the peak of prosperity for the Lancashire cotton industry and the Liverpool cotton market.

11. FIRST WARNINGS

With the opening of the twentieth century, business in Liverpool continued to flourish and the city developed in line with the quickening pace of life.

Although the usefulness of the canals had declined with the coming of the railway, in 1887 Manchester decided to become a port and the Manchester Ship Canal Company was formed. After buying the interests of the Bridgewater Navigation Company and Mersey–Irwell Navigation, work began on the present ship canal, which was opened in 1894, with wet and dry docks, wharfs and warehouses at Manchester. The canal is wide enough and deep enough for ocean-going merchant ships to pass right up from the Mersey estuary to Manchester for unloading.

At the turn of the century Britain was wealthy, busy and powerful, the centre of a vast empire, exporting manufactured goods and importing raw materials and food, and her docks were the largest in the world.

The trade union movement had been gathering power during the last years of the nineteenth century, and although wages were still low, the Edwardian era saw many social improvements, including the fixing of legal minimum wages in various industries. In 1909 the first old age pensions were awarded and in 1911 came the National Insurance Act.

In Liverpool, as the last of the old horse buses disappeared from the streets, many amenities were established, including the Liverpool Hospital for Consumption. In 1903 the University received its charter, although at this time it comprised only a few buildings on Brownlow Hill.

Bishop Chavasse had been appointed Bishop of Liverpool and it was largely through his inspiration that plans took shape for the long-awaited Anglican cathedral. The competition for the design was won by Sir Giles Scott, then a young man of twenty-three, and the site chosen was St James's Mount. King Edward VII laid the foundation stone in 1904 and the beautiful, red sandstone Gothic cathedral slowly took shape. The Lady Chapel was completed and consecrated in 1910, but at this point the architect changed his plan of a single transept with twin towers for a massive central tower, with east and west naves and a nave at the western end to balance the choir in the east.

Despite the extra cost involved, the committee accepted the new design and never regretted the alteration, for as the work continued they saw how magnificent the cathedral was going to be.

As the foundations of the cathedral were being laid, the old George dock was cleared, and in 1907 the offices of the Mersey Docks and Harbour Board were built. The following year the foundations were laid of the mighty Royal Liver building, the great tower block, surmounted by its four-faced clock and the two liver birds, which dominates the waterfront and is the welcoming landmark for home-coming Liverpool folk when they are still miles out at sea.

Liverpool's liver bird is a mystery, for no one quite knows what it is meant to be nor how it came to be incorporated in the city's coat of arms. In the language of heraldry, the Argent, or central silver shield of the coat of arms, is a "Cormorant in the beak a branch of seaweed called Laver all proper, and for the crest, on a wreath of the colours a Cormorant, the wings elevated, in the beak a branch of Laver proper".

In 1797 the addition of the figures of Neptune and a triton to the coat of arms was granted. "The Dexter Neptune with his sea-green mantle flowing, the waist wreathed with Laver; on his head an eastern crown gold; in his right hand his trident sable; the left supporting a banner of the arms of Liverpool; on the sinister a triton, wreathed as the dexter, and blowing his shell; the right hand supporting a banner, thereon a ship under sail in perspective all proper the banner-staves Or."

In the original crest surmounting the arms of the Common Seal, the bird was the eagle of St John, but during the siege of 1644 the original Common Seal of the Town was lost. A somewhat unskilful copy was later produced, in which the eagle looked more like a cormorant, and it is this strange creature which is now known as the Laver or Liver bird.

The most usual translation of the motto is "God has given this leisure to us", a sentiment which was to have a grim significance in the years to come, for with all the magnificence and grand building during the first decade of the twentieth century, all was not well in the wider realms of international politics and commerce.

Although in 1900 Britain could claim to be the wealthiest and most highly industrialized country in the world, other people were quickly awakening to the opportunities and demands of the new century.

Liverpool was the biggest importing raw cotton market and controlled the price of cotton throughout the world, but America, Japan and India were now entering into competition as cotton manufacturers, and America and several European countries were becoming serious rivals in other spheres as well, particularly coal and metals.

This was the beginning of the decline in British prosperity and supremacy. At the beginning of the nineteenth century Great Britain had a lead in the world metal trade, for the other great metal producing regions of the world had not yet been developed. Most of the world's supply of tin and copper came from Cornwall and large quantities of lead were mined in the Pennines. At first Britain had been able to export these metals, but as her manufactures absorbed an increasing amount of them there came a point where she found herself needing to import, and by this time other countries were developing their own resources, some, as in Malay, with British capital.

By 1900 the United States was the world producer of copper and lead, Malaya of tin and Germany of zinc. Cotton spinning was becoming more efficient in America, and Germany was well ahead in the light chemical and dyeing industries.

Yet in every field of industry Britain appeared to be expanding. We were using more wool and cotton, producing more coal and pig-iron. By 1911 there were more miners in England than agricultural labourers and our merchant fleet was increasing.

As wages rose, under pressure from the trade unions, more consumer goods were being sold and the retail trades were all prospering. Nevertheless, after 1873 our overall commercial position began to show signs of a depression. We both imported and exported more, for the population was steadily increasing, but the value of our exports began to decline in relation to imports, through competition from other countries. It was not a sudden collapse but a slow, corroding trend.

America's output of coal gradually outpaced Great Britain's. America and Germany both surpassed Great Britain's steel production and Belgium, Bohemia, Silesia and France proved themselves active competitors.

At the turn of the century few people saw anything significant when Lancashire began exporting second-hand textile machinery to Japan, India, China and the countries of Europe, but by 1906 several million pounds worth of new textile machinery were being sent to the new manufacturing centres, both from Great Britain and the United States. A few people saw that the trend held great potential dangers for Liverpool's cotton market and the Manchester industry, but during the gay days of Edwardian prosperity the mood was not right for forecasting gloom, nor could anyone have done much about it if they had.

Students from India and Japan arrived in Liverpool to learn the business of exporting textiles, but in those easy-going days they were regarded as valuable customers and were welcomed and entertained by the cotton merchants and their families. Before long other young men from East of Suez were appearing in even greater numbers in the technical colleges, provincial universities and night schools of the textile towns. They learnt a great deal about the modern textile business, though at first they were not good with machinery or at supervising large numbers of operatives. Very soon experienced senior operatives from the English textile mills were being invited to India, Japan, Hong Kong and Russia, at temptingly large salaries, to supervise the opening of new cotton factories, some in the heart of cotton-bearing regions.

The danger of real competition still seemed remote, for in Liverpool and Manchester the industry was booming and each year figures for both imports and exports rose. In 1907 the Liverpool cotton market imported 3,877,000 bales of cotton, nearly three million of which were from the United States and the rest from Brazil, Egypt, the West Indies and the East Indies. By 1911 the figure had risen to 5,230,399 bales, more than four and a quarter million from the United States. In 1913 the Gladstone dock, the biggest graving dock in the world, was built. On the Liverpool Cotton Exchange merchants were jubilant. The "futures" market was never more successful and in the warehouses there were large reserves, to ensure that the spinners and weavers of Manchester could receive regular supplies for months to come.

The Exchange was connected by a direct transatlantic cable with the New York Cotton Exchange and had by now thirty outside telephone lines, while every firm on the market was connected to the Exchange by a private telephone as well as a "ticker" system. All the cable companies had their offices in the Exchange and opening prices of cotton in the New York market were reproduced in every Manchester and Liverpool cotton office in three minutes, as well as the prices throughout the day, as they fluctuated with supply and demand.

Yet in the East cheap native labour was producing cotton cloth in increasing quantities, with Lancashire-made machinery, supervised by Lancashire-trained operatives, at a cost far below that of the Manchester cottons. The quality was not so good but it satisfied the market for which it was intended.

The other commercial activities of Liverpool were also flourishing in the years before 1914. Though the craft industries of pottery, clocks and watches had disappeared, the salt and sugar refineries continued to expand.

Liverpool had three groups of industries by now. The first group was concerned with shipping and the port. Ship-building and ship-repairing flourished on both sides of the estuary and there were numerous firms in Liverpool supplying ropes, tackle, flags, chronometers and similar nautical equipment. The business of marine insurance and banking, to cater for the needs of the importing and exporting merchants, was larger than in any city of the kingdom outside London.

The second group of industries was connected with bulky imports which could be processed more economically at the dockside, thereby saving heavy transport charges. These commodities included grain, sugar, timber, oilseed and tobacco. Merseyside had become the largest flour-milling centre in Europe, while the oilseed and tobacco-processing industries and the sugar refineries were among the most important in the country.

The third group of industries depended on the second, for they used the products of the sugar refineries and flour mills, and included the manufacture of biscuits, jams and jellies and sugar confectionery—Barker and Dobson, with their buttered brazils and Everton mints, having been established as early as 1834.

With the outbreak of the First World War Liverpool was busier than ever before, for Britain was no longer self-supporting in food and this was the end of our life-line across the Atlantic and the food supplies of the Americas. For a time German submarines haunted Liverpool Bay and the merchant ships, strangely camouflaged, would slip in and out of Liverpool, under cover of darkness whenever possible. A battalion of Liverpool men sailed off to the war in France and in 1917 American troops sailed in.

Losses to merchant shipping were terrible. In April 1917, at the worst time of the German U-boat campaign, more than a million tons of British and neutral shipping were sunk and one ship in every four leaving British ports was lost.

The price of cotton had begun to rise with the outbreak of war and now it increased sharply, for there was a threat of another cotton famine in Lancashire. However, the grave shortage of American cotton was supplemented by supplies of cotton through the Mediterranean from Egypt, and the industry kept going.

The following year came the Allied victories and the armistice. The victories were on land but Liverpool shipping played a vital part throughout those desperate war years in helping Great Britain to survive.

12. THE DEPRESSION

With the end of the First World War there was a short cotton boom, for war-time restrictions and shipping losses had caused a shortage of textiles throughout the world. Even China and India, with their own manufactures, needed the better quality Manchester textiles.

Liverpool now bought large quantities of American cotton to replenish her stocks. In the 1919–20 season the market bought nearly 4·5 million bales, of which more than 3·25 were from America. It was during this boom that Liverpool began seriously to tackle her housing problem and the great suburbs of Edge Lane, Lisburn Farm, Allerton and Queen's Drive were built. Then came the 680 acres of the Norris Green estate, with its 7,700 dwellings, its shops and churches, schools and cinemas.

Yet the post-war prosperity was very short-lived. As soon as the Eastern markets had bought all the Manchester cloth they needed for their immediate requirements, they fell back on the products of their own factories, which were steadily improving the quality and quantity of their output and entering the export market. Lancashire's great export trade in cloth and yarn to the Far East suddenly collapsed. Dozens of cotton mills closed and others went on short time.

It followed that American imports of raw cotton fell and the Liverpool Cotton Exchange suffered. In 1921 imports from America fell to 2·3 million bales and the price of raw cotton already in the Liverpool warehouses dropped rapidly. Merchants who had protected themselves with "futures" deals were saved from disaster, but the price of manufactured cloth fell even faster than that of raw cotton and merchants left with large stocks on their hands were ruined.

Within twelve months the price of stocks of cotton fell to a quarter of their original cost and the demand was halved. The years of the post-war depression had begun.

At the Peace Conference in 1919 the Allies had insisted that Germany must pay for the actual cost of the war, regardless of the fact that in order to do so she must reorganize her industries with money borrowed from the Allies and manufacture and export at the expense of the Allies' markets. The Allies seized £100 million of Germany's assets but within a few years Germany was borrowing back £50 million, mainly from the United States and Great Britain. Great Britain had lent millions of pounds to the Allies during the war and had herself borrowed heavily from the United States. Great Britain was prepared to cancel many of the Allies' debts but the United States insisted on full repayment from Great Britain.

Industries and businesses in Britain struggled to re-establish themselves in the world markets, but found that others were now taking their place. In Victorian times Britain's success had been based on relatively cheap goods made by cheap labour. Now the trade unions were insisting on higher wages. The price of British goods had to rise and they were undercut by foreign competitors.

With reduced demand for goods, there were very soon not enough jobs to go round in Britain and by July 1921, there were more than two and a half million unemployed. The situation improved a little during the later 1920s, but by 1930 it was nearly as bad as ever, with unemployment figures at well over two million again.

The whole country was affected, but the situation was worst in Lancashire, Yorkshire, Durham, Staffordshire and South Wales.

In 1930 a German historian wrote: "While British exports to all parts of the world have fallen, American have gone up. Where Germany has been driven from the field it has been to the advantage not of Britain, but of America—and Japan. While American industry expands, British industry, in its vital sections (coal, cotton) contracts. America has become the greatest financial magnate in the world."

By this time more than one in four of Liverpool's working people were idle and Merseyside had become a depressed area. The Cunard Company had to stop work on the *Queen Mary*, being built for them on Clydeside. With fewer goods being sold abroad, there was less money for imports. As Liverpool's wealth depended on her sea-borne trade and her industries on imports, the situation was desperate.

A victim of the depression

People who lived through these tragic years will never forget the utter hopelessness that haunted the faces of the men in the queues at the Employment Exchanges. Children were brought up in families which had never known the security of regular employment and a steady wage. The dole was enough to keep people alive but allowed for almost nothing beyond food and rent. The British Medical Association estimated that it cost a man with a wife and three children a minimum of 22s. 6d. a week for food and the rent of the worst slum tenement was an average of 6s. a week. Yet the maximum relief pay he could draw was 29s. 3d. The rent of the council houses was about double that of slum property, so people who had moved with such high hopes into trim new homes suffered all the more, and in places the death-rate through under-nourishment rose alarmingly.

The cost of living was also rising. Trade Unions demanded higher wages for those who were still in work. The Prime Minister, Mr Baldwin, argued that if wages were reduced more people could be employed. He recommended a 13·5 per cent cut in the wages of coal miners and longer working hours, for it had been found that three-quarters of the country's coal was being produced at a loss. The Trades Union Congress threatened strike action and on 3rd May 1926, the General Strike began, involving nearly four million miners and industrial workers. Nine days later it was called off, though the result was indecisive. The strike had cost the unions a vast amount of money and they had gained nothing. Unemployment increased and the dole queues grew longer.

In 1929 Labour won the general election with a small majority and Ramsay MacDonald became Prime Minister. Yet the depression grew worse. British manufacturing costs were the highest in the world and could not compete with the expanding industries of America, Germany, Italy, Japan and the Dominions.

Then came the world slump. It began in America. Twenty thousand American banks suspended payment and thousands of people found themselves suddenly penniless. Trade and industry were thrown into confusion and the United States were faced with ten million unemployed. The effect was quickly felt in Europe. In Germany five million men were thrown out of work; in Britain the unemployment figure rose to nearly three million.

Britain could not balance her budget and in 1931 Ramsay MacDonald resigned. An emergency National Government was formed with Ramsay MacDonald again Prime Minister

and Stanley Baldwin his second in command. By September of
that year Britain had to reduce the value of the pound, as there
was not enough gold and other assets in the vaults of the Bank
of England to balance the number of pound notes in circulation.

Drastic government economies had to be made. Wages and
salaries were reduced. Insurance contributions were increased
and benefits reduced. These were the years when Walter
Greenwood wrote his novel *Love on the Dole*, a bitter reflection
of life in Lancashire at this time, and the hunger marchers from
Jarrow, which had been one of the country's most important
shipyards, journeyed to London to protest after the yard was
dismantled, leaving eighty per cent of the population of the
town unemployed, with no hope of finding alternative work.

In Liverpool the situation grew steadily worse and by 1931
Lancashire had lost half her cotton textile trade. The Liverpool
City Council devised many means to try to ease matters.
Since the opening years of the century an increasing number of
people had chosen to live in Wirral and cross the Mersey each
day by the ferry, to reach their work in Liverpool. The queues
of vehicles at the goods ferry terminals at Birkenhead and
Liverpool were growing longer every year and it was obvious
that some new service must be devised.

A Mersey Co-ordination Committee was set up. At first
they considered the possibility of building a high-level bridge
across the Mersey but found that the cost would be exorbitant.
Moreover, many people were already predicting a second
World War and a bridge would have been a particularly
vulnerable bombing target. Eventually the City of Liverpool
and the Borough of Birkenhead joined in planning the Mersey
tunnel. The necessary Bill was passed through Parliament and
in 1925 work began.

From either bank of the river two pairs of tunnels were
drilled through the sandstone, one above the other. The lower
ones, which ultimately reached to a depth of nearly two
hundred feet below the river, were always in advance of the
upper ones and from them drillings were made both above and
ahead, to test the condition of the rock. When the engineers

were satisfied, drilling of the upper tunnels proceeded. They knew that near the Liverpool bank the rock would be thin; where necessary, it was reinforced with concrete.

When the two pairs of tunnels met, under the middle of the river, the space between them was demolished and the full-sized tunnel completed. The under-water part was lined with a vast iron tube and the under-land parts with concrete.

The roadway through the main tunnel, more than two miles long, is carried on two vertical walls and is thirty-six feet wide, with four traffic lanes. There are also two branch tunnels, with roadways nineteen feet wide, leading directly to the Liverpool and Birkenhead docks.

The tunnel cost nearly eight million pounds to build and was opened by King George V on 18th July, 1934. Apart from giving much needed employment to hundreds of Liverpool men it proved an inestimable boon, catering easily for the volume of traffic which was passing across the Mersey at this time.

During the excavations of the tunnel, one of the problems confronting the engineers was the disposal of the masses of red sandstone that had to be removed. Part of this was spread over land at Dingle, where the Mersey Docks and Harbour Board were working on a land reclamation scheme, to build the oil storage depot. Most of the remainder was taken to Otterspool, where a retaining wall was built along the river and where, many years later, the Otterspool promenade was built.

In addition to the tunnel, the Liverpool Corporation launched a large programme of further slum clearance and housebuilding and the Mersey Docks and Harbour Board began a huge dock improvement scheme.

These measures helped the unemployed but did not solve their ultimate problem. The City Council therefore decided on a policy of planned industrial development, building satellite townships and encouraging industrialists to bring their industries to the new settlements, where the labour force was already being established. Liverpool was the pioneer of this type of industrial estate, financed by the municipality.

In 1929 the Corporation bought the township of Speke, on its south-eastern boundary. They planned Speke not as an industrial site to which people would have to travel each day, but as a self-contained community, with its own shops and schools and other social and cultural amenities and homes for twenty-five thousand people, including houses with up to four bedrooms and garages, flats and old people's cottages. On the outskirts of the town 341 acres were set aside for industrial development and this area has since been extended by another hundred acres. The Liverpool Corporation Act of 1936 gave the Council the powers to buy and sell the land for industry, to build factories and lease, sell or advance mortgages on them.

A similar estate was planned at Fazakerley and about the same time a different type of industrial estate was acquired at Long Lane, Aintree. A certain amount of development on this 300 acres had already been undertaken by private industrialists but the Corporation now increased it—and with great success. At Aintree, industry is restricted to clean trades and today there are many model factories here for the preparation of various manufactured foods.

In the summer of 1939 negotiations were under way for the acquisition of the Kirkby Industrial Estate, but before they could be completed the outbreak of the Second World War put a stop to all further development for the next five years.

Work on the Anglican cathedral had been hindered during the 1914 war, but never completely halted, and in 1924 the cathedral was consecrated and the choir and eastern transept came into use for regular worship. This was the first time since the thirteenth century that a cathedral had been consecrated on an entirely new site. The following day the War Memorial Chapel and Cenotaph were dedicated, in memory of the men of Liverpool who had died during the First World War. Two years later the magnificent organ, said to be the largest church organ in the world, was dedicated.

The tower and the western transept were not yet built, but even during these years of grave industrial distress, money was raised by public appeal, and Lord Vestey and his brother, Sir

Liverpool Cathedral

Edmund, made munificent contributions, so that the work could continue.

With so much of the Anglican cathedral completed, the Roman Catholics felt an increasing urgency to build their own cathedral, for the diocese was very large. In 1930 the old workhouse on Brownlow Hill was sold by the Corporation, as the site of the Metropolitan Cathedral of Christ the King. The original design was by Sir Edward Lutyens, who planned a Byzantine cathedral, which, like the Anglican cathedral, was to be of red sandstone. The Lutyens design had a mighty dome, surmounted by a cross. The foundation stone was laid by Archbishop Downey in 1933 and for the next six years work proceeded.

It was in 1933 that the much loved old Philharmonic Hall was burned down, but the Philharmonic Society soon had plans under way for a new hall, which was built on the same site and opened in 1939.

But 1933 was also the year that Hitler became Chancellor of Germany and 1939 saw the outbreak of the Second World War.

13. LIVERPOOL RISES AGAIN

With the outbreak of the Second World War, Liverpool came into its own again. Once more, because of its geographical situation, facing the Atlantic, it was a vital port for ocean transport. It had the advantage of the sheltered Western Approaches, which were a measure of protection for shipping, although the city was to be as vulnerable to air attack as anywhere else in the British Isles.

By the end of August 1939, all the plans for the redevelopment of the docks, the slum clearance and the rehousing came to a halt, as Liverpool prepared yet again for war. Children and old people were sent away from the blacked-out city to the safety of the neighbouring countryside and many businesses also moved out with their reduced war-time staffs. During the winter of 1939 to 1940 convoys of ships sailed secretly and silently in and out of the port, laden with troops and supplies: few people shared the closely-guarded secret that in an operations room close to the old town hall in Dale Street, the Battle of the Atlantic was being directed. The industrial estates were turned swiftly over to wartime production and at Kirkby the Government established a vast Royal Ordnance factory, which changed 750 acres of agricultural land into an industrial area.

By the autumn of 1940 came the first German air raids. At the beginning they were intermittent. Then, just before Christmas, there were heavy raids for three nights in succession. This was the first German attempt to put both Liverpool and Manchester out of action. There was relative calm for the next few months but in the spring of 1941 came the tragic testing time. Liverpool suffered the most terrible week of sustained air attack. From 1st May to 8th May the Germans launched nightly bombing raids by repeated waves of aircraft, which followed each other at regular intervals, with a deadly inevitability, from nightfall to dawn.

The centre of Liverpool was destroyed. Many of the ancient, cherished landmarks were obliterated for ever. Hundreds of people were killed. Thousands were grievously injured. Even more were made homeless. When the *Malakand* was hit and blown up, the Huskisson Number 2 Branch Dock was wiped out. An ammunition train in Breckside siding caught fire and exploded, causing devastation throughout the entire district surrounding it. One of the Museum buildings was destroyed. The Parish Church was demolished, except for the tower.

"In the terrible raids of May, 1941—eight nights of repeated bombing . . . wide areas of the city were destroyed; 1,400 people were killed: thousands were injured; enormous fires raged, night and day, in the heart of the city, and at the docks. From Seaforth to Huskisson Dock the flames raged and burned, in ships, in warehouses, and in the dockside sheds; no less than 125,000 dwellings were damaged or destroyed. . . ."[1]

Yet the city survived. People recovered from the first shock. They adapted themselves, found temporary homes to replace those they had lost and went on working with renewed, grim determination. As in World War I, the work of Liverpool, both at the docks and in the factories, was vital to the survival of the country and, by the time the end came, in 1945, it was estimated that the port had handled seventy-five million tons of cargo, while 4,700,000 troops had passed through. Seventy-four thousand aeroplanes and gliders had been landed and the Battle of the Atlantic had been directed and won from the room in Dale Street.

Although so many plans for Liverpool and its people had to be temporarily shelved during the war, the work of creating the Anglican cathedral never stopped entirely. Even during the worst periods it went on, although with a greatly reduced labour force. In summer 1939 more than 250 men had been

[1] Quoted in the *Liverpool Raw Cotton Annual*, 1958 from "The Story of Liverpool", C. L. Lamb and L. Smallpage.

May 1941

working on the site but by 1945 there were only thirty-five.

In November 1940, after the first air raids, King George VI and Queen Elizabeth visited Liverpool, and to the cathedral authorities the King said: "Keep on with the work, if only in a small way. Refuse to be beaten." This they did, in the face of the severest setbacks. During the bombing of 1941 and 1942 the windows of the Lady Chapel and of the south wall of the Choir were blown out. The Lady Chapel was not fit for use again until 1955 but elsewhere the work went on and by July 1941, only two months after Liverpool's severest air raid, the vast central section of the cathedral was completed and in use. Before the end of the war the architect himself laid the last stone on the topmost pinnacle of the Vestey Tower.

The saddest and most moving corner of the cathedral is the beautiful cenotaph on which lies a book containing the names of the Liverpool men who died in both world wars, for by 1945 the number had reached nearly forty thousand.

From the economic and business point of view, Liverpool's most serious casualty during the war was the cotton market. Supplies of cotton were so small and their delivery so erratic that the Government took over the responsibility of the buying and distribution of all cotton supplies, and by March 1941, the "futures" market had closed. After the war, the Liverpool Cotton Association prepared once more for business and were dismayed when they received the news that the Government had appointed its own Raw Cotton Commission and intended to maintain responsibility for the importation, general distribution and maintenance of stocks, without the protection of the "futures" market, to hedge it against fluctuating prices. However, in 1954, with a change of government, the Liverpool Cotton Market was again opened, although by this time many of the old-established firms had gone out of business.

British markets for Lancashire cotton were still declining, particularly after 1952, and the Liverpool market never regained its former status. Today only about one and a half million bales of cotton, worth some £65 million, are imported by Liverpool each year, compared with the five and a half million in the peak year of 1911: and, like the woollen industry, the cotton industry has suffered from the competition of man-made fibres. In 1964, for example, although Great Britain exported £44·1 million of cotton yarn and woven cotton fabrics, mainly to Australia, South Africa, the Irish Republic and New Zealand, the exports of man-made fibre, yarns and woven fabrics was £58·5 million, being sent mainly to Sweden, South Africa, Australia, the Irish Republic and Switzerland.

The Cotton Exchange building has been reconstructed and converted into offices and the merchants have moved into these or others nearby. Nevertheless, the Liverpool cotton market is still important to the country's economy, for certain Liverpool firms carry on a large business in cotton which never reaches Liverpool. For example, a Liverpool firm may buy cotton in America and sell it to Japan. While the cotton goes directly across the Pacific, the profits from the deal come to the United Kingdom and are counted as an "invisible" but nonetheless valuable export.

Yet despite the remaining value of the cotton market, with the end of the war Liverpool faced the same problems that had beset her during the 1930s. The days of prosperity, based on the import and export of cotton, which had brought such flourishing business during the early years of the century, were over. Moreover, if Britain's overseas trade continued to decline, there would be increasing unemployment in Liverpool. The city looked to the future, and, to guard against this possibility, at once began to plan new industries, which have flourished and are still expanding.

During the last twenty-five years she has maintained her position as one of the world's greatest seaports and the largest exporting port of the Commonwealth, as well as an international centre of banking, commerce and insurance. And at the same time she has become one of Britain's most important industrial areas, the products of her vast industrial estates making vital contributions to the country's exports.

Today Liverpool's principal exports are manufactured goods, iron and steel, vehicles, chemicals, textiles, salt and machinery. The main imports are petroleum, grain, ores, non-ferrous metals, sugar, wood, oils, fruit and cotton. In all, she handles more than 25,300,000 tons of cargo each year at her seven miles of docks and thirty-seven miles of quays.

The 1960s saw the rapid rise of Merseyside's car manufacturing industry, with Ford, Vauxhall and British Leyland factories all established. Ford's huge plant was built at Halewood in 1963 and today is employing 14,000 workers, producing 1,300 vehicles and 3,000 gear-boxes a day, half of which are for export. Ford's are now, in the summer of 1970, one of Liverpool's biggest industrial employers. British Leyland, which opened at Speke with the manufacture of motor-car components, is now planning to make complete vehicles and will ultimately employ 4,000 men.

Liverpool's light engineering works produce anything from telephones to billiard tables, electric cables to refrigerators. The flour mills of Merseyside are still the largest in Europe. Sugar-refining employs 5,000 people. Other industries are tanning, the manufacturing of cattle foods, soap, paper and paint, and tobacco blending. The Dunlop rubber factory produces all manner of goods, from industrial belting to golf balls. Confectionery and biscuits are still important manufactures, the factories being close to the sugar refineries, and within the last few years Liverpool has been producing some excellent colour printing and has also established a pharmaceutical and biochemical industry.

The port is developing and expanding each year, an increasing amount of cargo being handled in vast containers, which save labour costs in transport. The great Seaforth project to provide a new port area with three container berths as well as ten modern deep-water berths for general cargo is nearly completed and will be joined to the Gladstone Container Berth, which was designed as a temporary measure while the Seaforth dock, with its mile of frontage, was being built.

The Tranmere Oil Terminal takes 200,000-ton oil tankers and a project is being considered for a man-made island to be constructed eleven miles off the Welsh coast, in Liverpool Bay, to serve as a terminal for the million-ton tankers of the future. It is to be 3,800 feet long with vast storage tanks and will be connected with the mainland by two underwater pipes.

The cranes and hoists for Liverpool's cargo are on a gargantuan scale. At the Gladstone dock fifty-ton cranes are being used with mechanical hoists for lifting and stacking the containers. Spacious transit sheds, wide quays and speedy handling of cargoes are fast turning Liverpool and Birkenhead into Europe's main Atlantic seaport.

At the end of 1951 it was estimated that, during the year, six million vehicles had passed through the Mersey tunnel between Liverpool and Birkenhead. By 1969 the figure had risen to seventeen million and peak-hour traffic had reached saturation point. To relieve the congestion a second tunnel is now being built between Liverpool and Wallasey.

In 1961 the Liverpool Corporation took over the airport at Speke from the Ministry of Aviation and it is now one of the most up-to-date in the United Kingdom. It is only six miles from the city centre, with easy access to Preston, Manchester, Runcorn and the Mersey tunnel and has regular air services to most of the important towns and cities of Britain and to many on the Continent.

A few years after the war ended it was reported that Liverpool still had 80,000 slum houses, a survival of the bad old days of the Victorian mushroom growth. These are no longer tolerated. Street by street, they are being cleared away and the occupants rehoused. The City Council is rebuilding the whole of the centre of the city, providing what has been described as the largest pedestrian precinct outside Venice, and has embarked on a redevelopment scheme which will take fifteen years to complete.

Liverpool will then be a proud and beautiful city, despite all the controversy now raging about the new architecture. It already has buildings which compare with the best in Europe. The magnificent and elegant St George's Hall, considered to be the finest example of the Graeco-Roman style of architecture in Europe, was unscarred by the war. The museums, rebuilt after the war damage, the Walker Art Gallery and the Central Libraries, all in the style of the Classical revival, form a noble complex of buildings. The blocks of offices on the water front, the solid, straight-sided, soaring slab of the Royal Liver building, with its domes and twin towers, surmounted by the Liver birds, the Docks and Harbour Board, with its Byzantine dome and Florentine façade, and the Cunard building are all grandiose and impressive. The little Parish Church of Our Lady and St Nicholas, close by, on the site of seven hundred years of continuous worship, has been rebuilt.

In 1948 work was resumed on the nave of the Anglican cathedral. Between 1950 and 1960 enough money was raised to build the first bay of the nave. By 1967 the second was completed and work had begun on the third bay. The design for the west front had to be modified because of expense, but in essentials the result is similar to the east front, with a high arch enclosing a great window, deeply recessed, and flanked by two buttresses: and it is hoped that the work will be completed in 1975.

Liverpool cathedral is beautiful in every detail, from the carving of the English oak choir stalls to the enchanting little stone angels, and the impression as one enters is of lofty spaciousness and a holy calm. High up across the nave is a wooden bridge where you can stand, half way between the floor and the roof, in intimacy with the very fabric of the building, surrounded by the warm, dark red sandstone, against which the magnificent gilding of the reredos and the high altar glitters triumphantly.

When war broke out in 1939 little progress, beyond the foundations, had been made with the long-awaited Roman Catholic cathedral. After the war, the Lutyens' plan was abandoned and in 1960 an international competition for a new design was held. It was won by Frederick Gibberd and building began in October 1962. By the end of 1966 the structural work was mostly completed and the high altar was consecrated in May 1967.

This is the most modern cathedral in Britain and a complete contrast to Lutyens' Byzantine plan and to Scott's Gothic Anglican cathedral. The Metropolitan Cathedral of Christ the King is circular, composed of sixteen reinforced concrete blocks which enclose a circular nave large enough to seat a congregation of two thousand people, and the high altar, a solid block of Macedonian white marble, is in the centre. The cathedral has a conical roof of concrete slabs, covered with

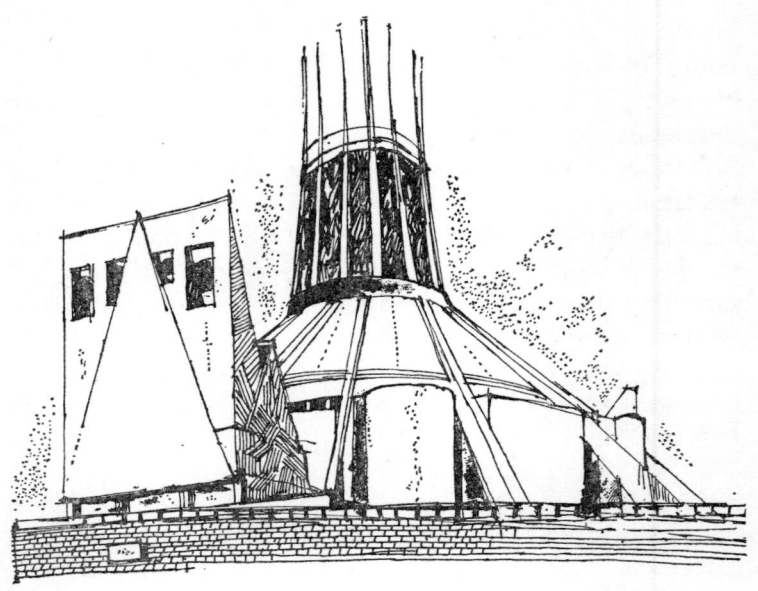

Liverpool Metropolitan Cathedral of Christ the King

aluminium, which tapers into a tower filled with brilliantly
coloured glass, shining at night-time like a vast lantern: and the
tower is surmounted by sixteen pinnacles, soaring to the sky
like a mighty crown.

In addition to the Chapel of the Blessed Sacrament, a Lady
Chapel and a Baptistry, the cathedral has eight small chapels, all
of which lead from the nave.

The exterior, rising to a height of nearly three hundred feet,
is so unorthodox that at first sight it is strangely disturbing. It
has been described as a giant hop kiln or an inverted concrete
funnel. It contrasts aggressively with the surrounding buildings, but at night-time it is beautiful, the lights from the great
lantern shining out across the city: and the stark simplicity of
the grey and white stone interior, with the intense blue light
from the glass which surrounds the sixteen walls in narrow
bands, has most marvellously created an atmosphere of sanctity
and timelessness, belonging to the future but rooted in the past.

This is Liverpool today—a magnificent port and a commercial and industrial city, busy and expanding, with churches and

cathedrals, civic buildings, libraries and museums of which the city is justly proud. Yet it is far more than all this. It is a young people's city, with an abounding vitality, and the influences of its rich cultural life spread far afield.

Liverpool has the largest percentage of young people under twenty-five of any city in the country, people born since the end of World War II, who are the children of the post-war social revolution.

The opportunities for their education are improving all the time. When Liverpool University was founded in 1881 it had ninety-three students. Today it has more than 6,000 and during the 1970s the number is expected to reach 10,000. The Liverpool School of Medicine, now part of the university, has become one of the most important centres in the world for the study of tropical diseases. It was founded in 1898, at the instigation of Alfred Lewis Jones, who was then chairman of the West African Trade section of the Liverpool Chamber of Commerce. At the time it was the first of its kind and since those days the school has made studies in many other parts of Africa and also throughout the Middle East and the Pacific.

In addition to the university, Liverpool has four major colleges for advanced education—the colleges of Technology, Commerce, Building and Art—as well as many other colleges for school-leavers, where they can receive technical, commercial and other vocational training so vitally important for their ultimate welfare. Here, too, those who have missed their place in the mainstream of education, during their earlier years, have a chance to catch up.

Most of the young people of Liverpool know what they want and can shout loud enough to get it, or somewhere near it, but despite all the social amenities now offered them, they have their problems. There is unemployment, and wages are below the national average. During the summer of 1970 the unemployment rate for the north-west was 2·8 per cent compared with 2·7 per cent for the country as a whole, largely because the cotton industry now employs 10,000 fewer than in 1960 and the Lancashire coalfield is declining, while on

Merseyside, beset by labour disputes, the unemployment figure was 4·1 per cent.

Yet these troubles have not diminished the astonishing and spontaneous burst of artistic creation of the last ten or fifteen years. In the entertainment and cultural field, Liverpool has become famous not only for its comics, its two splendid rival football teams and its race-course, but for its poets, artists and pop singers. Of these it was the pop groups, particularly the Beatles, which brought Liverpool suddenly into the national headlines.

Writing of the Mersey sound in his book *Art in the City*, John Willett says: "Commercialized as it quickly became, this was a spontaneous form of popular music that developed in clubs and cellars all over Liverpool at the end of the 1950s: small groups of very young, very un-slick and apparently un-professional musicians shouting and pounding out their tunes on electric guitars. The four Beatles were at first only one of the wildest and toughest of these; they came together in 1960, were top of the local popularity poll in 1961, started recording for EMI in 1962, then became a national institution the next year and a world-wide craze during 1964. Since then they have been pushed out of the top place in the national popularity charts by groups from other parts of the country, but they still stand in many people's minds for a special kind of Liverpool vitality. . . . 'The Beatles are the best thing that has happened to Liverpool', the painter Adrian Henri told me. He was not thinking only of the noise they make."

There was something endearingly ingenuous about the Beatles when they first came to the public eye and ear. They seemed to be slightly startled at their own success and did not appear to take themselves as seriously as their promoters did. For several years they were undoubtedly the most talented and original of the pop groups and some of their songs and lyrics may well outlast them, for they have become as popular in America and the rest of the world as in Great Britain.

Dozens of rhythm and blues groups sprang up in Liverpool throughout the sixties, most of them highly original and owing

Beatles John Lennon and Paul McCartney, 1970

little to accepted musical forms. They were, says John Willett, "a fresh wave of young Liverpuddlians, bright products of the post-war state school system, who had found their own way of expressing themselves without any noticeable advice or encouragement from anybody else. With their special brand of anarchy, aggressive yet human, they were just one jump ahead of their contemporaries. . . ."

Edward Lucie-Smith in *The Liverpool Scene*, describing this explosion of post-war talent, says: "Such torrents of drivel have been written about pop music, pop culture and pop art since the advent of the Beatles that one is reluctant to take the whole subject up again. Yet there are one or two things which seem to me worth noticing. For example, the fact that the success of the Beatles had a seismic effect on provincial culture as a whole. For the first time London had been left out in the cold till the very last minute. The upsurge of the groups went on for a long time after the Beatles had established themselves as international idols. The journalists and the investigators came, and entertainers in Liverpool were suddenly provided with an acceptable identity."

Today amongst the prodigious number of cafés, pubs,

betting shops, cut-price stores, clothes shops, discothèques and drink and dance clubs there are some three hundred music pop groups in Liverpool, meeting mostly in clubs and cellars, the most famous being the Cavern, the home of the Mersey beat: and accommodation for eighty beat clubs is being planned for the new City Centre.

As early as 1947 the first Music Box was founded and now there are six of these meeting places for young people between fourteen and twenty-five, who want to make a cheerful noise.

Along with the pop groups appeared the Liverpool poets, their work reflecting sympathetically the way of life and thought of contemporary Liverpool. This poetry, breaking away from traditional forms, is as spontaneous as the music of the pop groups and because of its emotional impact poetry readings have as ready audiences.

Edward Lucie-Smith says of the poems he has chosen for his anthology *The Liverpool Scene*: ". . . they seem to me to be written by people who are more interested in life than litera-ture. Sentimentality, coarseness of texture, carelessness with details—all of these are things which are present in full measure. What the reader has to decide for himself is whether these form an insuperable barrier to enjoyment. Even at their most casual and surrealist, these poets always give the impression of being real people at grips with real and pressing situations. Theirs is not the only sort of poetry one can write, but at least it seems to me a poetry which is worth reading, and which seems to fore-shadow developments which are bound to take place in both our literature and our society as a whole."

Brian Patten, Adrian Henri, Spike Hawkins and Roger McGough have all received national recognition as poets of distinction and in Liverpool Adrian Henri's poetry readings are attended enthusiastically. Originally a painter, he has worked with pop groups in presenting his "events" or stage "happen-ings" at the Hope Hall and the Cavern, and both he and Patten have experimented in reading their verse to the accompaniment of pop music.

Painting and sculpture are related to pop music in a similar way. Arthur Dooley, the sculptor, for example, has shown the pop groups the analogy between his own form of expression and theirs.

Arthur Dooley is one of the best known Liverpool sculptors but there are several doing interesting work in wood, metal and stone, as well as a number of very talented artists, though for the most part they have to rely on teaching or some other employment for a living. Several are teachers at the College of Art. A few sell their paintings in London and some to local patrons, but sales are not large and there is no recognizable Liverpool style of painting as yet, comparable with the poetry and pop music.

However, the Liverpool Academy is a thriving institution with eighty members and associates, nearly all of them local and professional.

The Merseyside Arts Association, formed in 1969, has 120 member societies, with 150 poets and more than 200 artists on its files. As well as providing lectures and concerts in the city, they take them to the surrounding districts, thereby creating new audiences. In May 1970, a tour of writers sponsored by the Arts Council, which included Nell Dunn, John Bowen, Adrian Henri and Peter Buckman, made more than sixteen visits to Merseyside, speaking at libraries, colleges and schools, and in the same year Harold Hikins, the Merseyside librarian-poet, organized poetry readings throughout the region, forestalling the critics by calling his touring group, "Harold Hikins Famous Merseyside Arts Association Poetry Circus".

The Royal Liverpool Philharmonic Orchestra, Ballet For All, Opera For All and Northern Dance Theatre are also making short tours.

With all these increasing opportunities, the people of Liverpool have become deeply interested in the arts. The Royal Liverpool Philharmonic Orchestra is world-famous and has paid many visits to Europe, while a number of distinguished European conductors have come to Liverpool.

The Philharmonic Hall, home of the orchestra, was rebuilt in 1939 and is probably the most important of the provincial concert halls. Many new works are heard here for the first time. In 1946, for example, the late Sir Malcolm Sargent conducted the first performance of Benjamin Britten's *Young Person's Guide to the Orchestra*. Concerts arranged especially for the works and business houses are also held. These "industrial" concerts are so popular that they draw audiences of 6,000 and even then tickets have sometimes to be drawn from a hat, as the demand exceeds the supply. The Christmas carol concerts and the performances of the *Messiah* draw equally large audiences, for music booms in Liverpool.

Nowadays nearly every child learns to play some kind of musical instrument at school and there are plenty of opportunities for them to use their skills. Many schools have their own orchestras, from which they can try for entry to the Merseyside Youth Orchestra: and for the cleverest, this is a step towards the National Youth Orchestra. The Liverpool Youth Music Festival has about 1,400 entrants each year and there are three Youth Choirs in the city, each a hundred strong, as well as a Liverpool Youth Band. From the Youth Chorus the members can graduate to the Liverpool Philharmonic Choir or the Liverpool Welsh Choral Union, while the university has its choir and orchestra performing both chamber music and oratorios.

For the connoisseurs, the Bluecoat Chambers, the elegant eighteenth-century building which once housed the school, has become a fascinating cultural centre. It has a concert hall for chamber music and also suites of studios as well as a workshop where clavichords and harpsichords are made. It is the headquarters of forty-six organizations, nineteen of which are concerned entirely with music: for example, the Verdi Society, the Liverpool Grand Opera Company, the Liverpool Opera Circle, the Renaissance Music Group, the Lieder Circle and the Liverpool Music Group.

There are four professional theatres in the city, the Royal Court, the Empire, the Playhouse and the Everyman, as well as the Neptune Theatre, where amateur groups have an opportunity to perform. For a time the Royal Court was turned over to bingo but the theatre lovers of Liverpool petitioned the Council, firmly and successfully, to buy it back, so that it could be used for its proper purpose.

Nowhere is the vitality of Liverpool more evident than at the Everyman Theatre where, during the last few years, its talented company has determined, with gratifying success, to make drama an important part of the cultural life of the city, not only for adults, but also for schoolchildren. The theatre had a grim struggle in the early days, but now, with grants from the Liverpool City Council and the Arts Council of Great Britain, it can report that its finances are in a stable condition.

In Victorian times the building in Hope Street was a non-conformist chapel. Since 1967 it has gradually been transformed into a comfortable, modern theatre, but now it is hardly large enough for its steadily increasing audiences. The small, regular company of players are not particularly well paid as yet, but are fast making a name for themselves, not only in Liverpool and the north-west, but throughout the whole country.

The theatre puts on a wide choice of plays and the list for the last two or three years includes Shakespeare, some of the Restoration comedies, Molière, Sheridan, Ibsen, Chekhov and Shaw. In between the classics there have been comedies such as *Hobson's Choice* and *Charley's Aunt* and modern plays such as Peter Nicholls' *A Day in the Death of Joe Egg*, Eugene O'Neill's *A Touch of the Poet*, David Halliwell's *Little Malcolm and His Struggles Against the Eunuchs* and Paul Ableman's *Green Julia*. Amongst first productions were *The Two-Backed Beast* by David Selbourne and *The Commission* by Roger McGough.

As the report on the progress of the theatre says: "The criterion for choosing a play is that it must be a good play in its own right. We would call ourselves 'experimental' not because we do a great deal of new work (which can be done in a very old-fashioned way), but because we bring experiment to the production of the plays." And this includes the production of classical plays, which the company try to make clear and relevant to modern audiences.

The theatre also produces documentary plays, as for example *The Slave Trade* and *The Liverpool Funnel*, and one written to celebrate the opening of the Metropolitan cathedral.

These documentaries are extremely popular with the school-children, with whom an important part of the theatre's work is concerned. In the afternoons plays are put on especially for them. They are not necessarily plays written specifically for children, but plays which it is thought they will enjoy and understand. Some are part of the schools' syllabus, but many are plays of general interest which are also shown at the evening performances.

At these matinées key scenes of plays are sometimes acted and followed by a discussion between the children and players on the interpretation and production. The Department of Education and Science is particularly interested in extending this work and the teachers are co-operating. Members of the company visit certain schools to help them with their own drama and dramatic interpretations. Children studying a certain project will improvise and act relevant documentary episodes, in addition to their reading and other work on the subject, and the theatre's director of the Schools' Work is turning increasingly from the scripted play to this kind of group work and spontaneous improvisation. The theatre also runs drama courses for teachers, to help them with the techniques of classroom improvisation.

The Company tours plays throughout the north-west and each year takes its Christmas play to the Anglican cathedral for three nights. The theatre has experimented with a season of Late Night Films, run as a club, choosing films which are distinguished but unlikely to be shown in the commercial cinemas of the city because of their relatively limited appeal.

When the Everyman company is not performing, the theatre is on hire to amateur players, folk groups, music societies and poets. From time to time there are visiting companies. *The Scaffold* and the *Merseyside Unity Theatre* have on occasion taken the theatre for complete weeks and art exhibitions, including children's work, have been held in the auditorium, the first being devoted to the work of the Liverpool artist Sam Walsh.

The Everyman receives an annual grant from the Liverpool City Council, which pays the rent; the Arts Council gives a revenue grant; and for the schools' performances the Liverpool, Lancashire and Bootle Education Authorities subsidize the children's seats.

The Playhouse has a substantial grant from the Arts Council, which enables its director to present new plays as well as great modern plays and classics, and of the Everyman Theatre he recently said: "We are particularly fortunate in having this theatre which is dedicated to experiment and which has received a national reputation in a very short time as the birthplace of very exciting work. Its policy can be a tremendously exciting contrast to the policy here."

The museums and art gallery of Liverpool are as alive and vigorous as the theatres. The city museum attracts more than half a million visitors a year, not only to its permanent collection, but to the special exhibitions it presents from time to time, and to its new transport museum, planetarium, coffee bar and cinema, which has been installed in the last coach of the old Liverpool Elevated, now in the transport museum.

The Walker Gallery, as popular as the museum, ranks as one of the four most important provincial art collections in the country and holds special exhibitions based on its reserve collection, which includes many of the large Victorian narrative pictures and a collection of English sporting paintings. There is a special space set aside in the gallery for contemporary art exhibitions, many of the pictures being by Liverpool artists.

This brings Liverpool's story up to 1970—a story of seven hundred years of steady achievement in face of much poverty and suffering, as well as national disasters and conflicts. The prospects for the future are bright. A magnificent city is being created for her people and they have the vigour and quick intelligence to grasp their new and long overdue opportunities and enjoy them to the full.

FURTHER READING

ALLISON, J. E., *The Mersey Estuary* (Liverpool U.P., 1949).

BAINES, T., *History of the Commerce and Town of Liverpool* (Longman, 1852).

BROOKE, R., *Liverpool as it was during the Last Quarter of the Eighteenth Century, 1775 to 1800* (Mawdsley and Son, Liverpool and Russell Smith, London, 1853).

BURFORD, P. (Ed.), *A Guide to Merseyside* (Pyramid Press, 1961).

CARLSON, ROBERT E., *The Liverpool and Manchester Railway Project* (David and Charles, Newton Abbot, 1969).

CHANDLER, G., *Liverpool* (Batsford, 1957).

CHANDLER, G., *Liverpool Shipping* (Phoenix House, 1960).

CHANDLER, G. and SAXTON, E. B., *Liverpool Under James I* (Liverpool City Council, 1960).

City of Liverpool Official Handbook (Liverpool City Council, n.d.).

City of Liverpool Official Industrial Handbook (Burrows, n.d.).

HARRIES, W. T., *Landmarks in Liverpool History* (G. Philip and Son, 1946).

HERDMAN, W. G., *Pictorial Relics of Ancient Liverpool*, 2 vols. (H. Graves and Co., 1878).

LAMB, C. L. and SMALLPAGE, E., *The Story of Liverpool* (Daily Post Printer, 1946).

LUCIE-SMITH, EDWARD, *The Liverpool Scene* (Carroll, 1967).

MACHIN, W. F., "A Short History of the Liverpool Cotton Market", *Liverpool Raw Cotton Annual* (Turner, Routledge and Co. Ltd., Liverpool, 1957–8).

MACKENZIE-GRIEVE, A., *The Last Years of the English Slave Trade, 1750–1807* (Putnam, 1941).

MERSEY DOCKS AND HARBOUR BOARD, *Business In Great Waters*, *1958* (published for the Board by Newman Neame).

MUIR, J. R., *History of Liverpool* (Williams and Norgate; Liverpool U.P., 1907).

MUIR, J. R. and PLATT, E. M., *History of Municipal Government in Liverpool, from the Earliest Times to the Municipal Reform Act of 1835* (Liverpool U.P., 1906).

PARKINSON, C. N., *The Rise of the Port of Liverpool* (Liverpool U.P., 1952).

PEET, H., *Liverpool in the Reign of Queen Anne, 1705 and 1708* (H. Young, 1908).

PICTON, SIR J. A., *Municipal Archives and Records* (*1207–1835*), 2 vols. (G. G. Walmsley, 1883–1886).

PICTON, SIR J. A., *Memorials of Liverpool*, 2 vols. (Edward Howell, 1903).

SMITH, W., *Distribution of Population and the Location of Industry on Merseyside* (Liverpool U. P., 1942).

SMITH, W. (Ed.), *A Scientific Survey of Merseyside* (published for British Association for the Advancement of Science by Liverpool U.P., 1953).

TOUZEAU, J., *The Rise and Progress of Liverpool, from 1551 to 1835*, 2 vols. (Liverpool Booksellers Co. Ltd., 1910).

TRAVIS, W. G., *Flora of South Lancashire* (Ed. J. P. Savidge) (Liverpool Botanical Society, 1963).

TWEMLOW, J. A., *Liverpool Town Books: (1550–1603)*, 2 vols. (Univ. of Liverpool—School of Local History, 1918–35).

Victoria History of the County of Lancaster, ed. by W. Farrer and J. Brownbill, vols. 3–4 (Constable, 1907–11).

WHITE, B. D., *History of the Corporation of Liverpool, 1835–1914* (Liverpool U.P., 1952).

WILLETT, JOHN, *Art in the City* (Methuen, 1967).

WILLIAMS, G., *History of the Liverpool Privateers and Letters of Marque; with an account of the Liverpool Slave Trade* (Heinemann, 1897).

INDEX